Digital Marketing

A MANAGING DIRECTOR'S GUIDE

Digital Marketing

A Managing Director's Guide

OLGA TRAVLOS

Olga Travlos
Xanthos Limited
Unit 2 Clive Court
Bartholomew's Walk
Cambridgeshire Business Park
Ely
Cambridgeshire
CB7 4EA

www.e-xanthos.co.uk

Photo credit: Mark Ashworth

First published in the United Kingdom in 2018 by Xanthos Limited:

ISBN 978-1-9164081-3-5

THANKS AND ACKNOWLEDGEMENTS

Thanks to Jim McLaughlin who inspired me to write this book and Ian Rowland and Vicki Utting who helped me realise the book. Thanks also to Adam Barsby, Ajith Laxman and Peter Laborne for their contributions and, of course, the Xanthos customers without whom this book would not have been possible. As always, thanks to my husband for his unswerving support.

ABOUT THE AUTHOR

 Olga Travlos is an e-commerce and digital marketing strategist. She is the founder and managing director of Xanthos, an agency that specialises in digital marketing and e-commerce for small- and medium-sized companies. She has many years senior management experience in a number of industries in the private sector.

"Olga Travlos is a very proficient adviser who has delivered great results and substantial added value for our business. Her SEO work propelled our website to the top of the Google rankings for the keywords that mattered to us, and the customer services that she provided during the setup of our e-commerce site has been truly outstanding. Her proactive stance in identifying our business needs and in finding practical solutions to our stringent requirements has made all the difference."

Olivier Picard, Managing Director
ISC Medical

"As a strategic partner of over ten years, Xanthos have been fundamental to our long term digital marketing performance. Their SEO, paid search, marketing automation, content marketing and e-commerce services, along with their deep-rooted understanding of our business and market place, has enabled us to take market share from our competitors and to ride a wave of rapid growth. The forward-thinking strategies that Xanthos deploy have

enabled me to focus my team on winning strategies that drive performance through all stages of the marketing funnel."

James Warren, Head of Digital Marketing
IT Governance Ltd

ABOUT XANTHOS

Xanthos is a digital marketing agency that specialises in helping small- and medium-sized businesses increase their profits through the strategic development and implementation of digital marketing.

We work with managing directors and CEOs of small- and medium-sized businesses who know that digital marketing is key to their business success. We are committed to gaining an understanding of each client's specific business need. We couple this with our expertise in digital marketing to generate results that make a significant, positive difference to each client's business.

We have also devised a Digital Marketing Quotient to help managing directors and CEOs evaluate the digital marketing standing of their businesses. You can access this here:

https://www.e-xanthos.co.uk/digital-marketing-quotient

We also design and build websites for businesses, with particular strength in e-commerce websites customised to meet specific market needs.

You can stay up to date with the latest developments in digital marketing by signing up to our newsletter:

https://www.e-xanthos.co.uk/newsletter

CONTENTS

Introduction 1
Chapter 1: Survive and thrive in the digital age 5
    What is 'digital marketing'? 5
    Wasted opportunities 6
Chapter 2: Website insight 9
    Your website is only the start 9
    Keeping your website up to date 9
    Types of change 16
    Content management systems 18
    Your website budget 20
Chapter 3: Cyber security and data protection 23
    Threat and defence 23
    General Data Protection Regulation (GDPR) 24
    Practical examples 32
    What next? 35
    Privacy and Electronic Communications Regulations
    (PECR) and EU ePrivacy Regulation (ePR) 36
Chapter 4: Digital marketing strategy 41
    Creating a DM strategy 41
Chapter 5: Search engine optimisation (SEO) 55
    In search of higher rankings 55
    Where to start 64
    Architecture 71
    Google position zero 76
    Schema markup 79
    Off-page optimisation 85
Chapter 6: Content is king 93
    What is content marketing? 93
    Email newsletter 95
    Whitepapers 95

Contents

Ebooks 95
Case studies 96
Webinar 96
Video 96
Podcasts 98
Infographics 98
Online surveys 100
Online press releases 100
Chapter 7: Social media marketing 103
Valuable opportunities 103
Examples of social media marketing 105
Campaigns 124
Open graph tags 127
Summary 128
Chapter 8: Email or fail 131
Email and ROI 131
List acquisition 131
Email campaigns 135
Subject lines 138
Personalisation 139
Landing pages 140
Mobile 140
Test, measure and refine 140
Email marketing platforms 145
Chapter 9: It's wise to advertise 147
The rise and rise of paid advertising 147
Google AdWords 147
Search ads 148
Keyword research 148
Match type 149
Example strategies 150
Writing your ad 151
Budget 154

Contents

Display ads 155
Combined targeting 159
Test, measure and refine 159
Google Shopping Ads 159
Amazon ads 160
Facebook ads 162
Google v Facebook 164
Chapter 10: The fun of funnels 169
Why automate? 169
Conversion funnels 169
Funnel example 171
Chapter 11: Treasure the measure 173
The joy of data 173
Google Analytics 173
Conversion rate optimisation 179
Chapter 12: Outsource? Of course! 189
A new profession 189
Case studies 197
About Xanthos 199

INTRODUCTION

In 2000, when the internet was still young, I developed the IT strategy for a FTSE 250 company. This necessarily involved trying to assess the impact of the internet. In my research, I came across the then-fledgling Amazon. In their early years, they managed to take 30% of Barnes and Noble's market share — and Barnes and Noble didn't see it coming. I knew then that the internet was going to transform business.

I also read an interview with Jean-Paul Garnier, then CEO of Smith Kline Beecham (SKB). He told the story of his son starting a business and selling it six months later for $1 million. Garnier said SKB could take six months just to organise a meeting to *start* discussing what they could do online. It was clear to me that large businesses would take a long time to devise their online strategy while small- and medium-sized businesses, being more agile and flexible, could get a head start. However, I realised they would need help to do this, which is why I set up Xanthos Digital Marketing in 2002.

Since those early days, things have become rather complicated. Back in 2002, once I had talked to a client about websites and search engine optimisation (SEO), that was pretty much all I had to take care of for them.

Then the landscape changed. SEO became easier for businesses to manage themselves (provided they had a good website and knew how to make it search-engine friendly).

Then Google started Google AdWords.

Then Social media erupted.

Meanwhile, email marketing was quietly establishing itself as a killer marketing tool.

These and many other changes made life difficult for businesses. They were trying to concentrate on their core competencies while *also* maintaining an effective website *and* implementing their online marketing. Not many businesses wanted to spend all day wrestling with ever-changing internet jargon, complex software packages and digital marketing techniques (and I can't blame them).

As the internet continued to evolve, more businesses realised the smart solution: they decided to focus on growing their business and to outsource their digital marketing to a specialist agency. This is clearly the more practical option and makes good business sense. You would expect me to say this, given that I run such an agency, but it's nonetheless true!

However, even when you outsource your digital marketing, you need to be an *educated* customer so you can understand what your agency is actually doing for you. Being an *informed* client means you can contribute ideas and get more out of your agency — with correspondingly greater benefits for your business.

This is why I've written this guide. It is specifically aimed at managing directors and CEOs of small- to medium-sized businesses. I want you to understand what digital marketing *is*, in the simplest and clearest terms, so that you can work with your agency to achieve the best results for your business.

You can read it end-to-end or just dip into various chapters as required.

Introduction

Welcome to Digital Marketing: A Managing Director's Guide.

CHAPTER 1: SURVIVE AND THRIVE IN THE DIGITAL AGE

What is 'digital marketing'?

When the internet first started being used for commercial purposes, the term 'internet marketing' referred to marketing a website on the internet. As the technology advanced and broadband became widespread, people simply referred to 'being online'. More recently, with the rise of smartphones, social media and online video, the term 'digital marketing' has come into use. I will refer to 'digital marketing' and 'online marketing' interchangeably.

Digital marketing includes:

- Websites.
- Search Engine Optimisation (SEO).
- Online PR.
- Content marketing.
- Social media marketing.
- Email marketing.
- Paid advertising.
- Marketing automation.
- Analysis and measurement.

In the past, most businesses generated new business leads through:

- Telemarketing.
- Yellow Pages advertising.

- Newspaper advertising.
- Trade magazine advertising.
- Traditional PR.
- Exhibitions.
- Billboards.
- Salespeople.
- Radio advertising.

A half-page colour advert in the Yellow Pages used to cost from £5K per annum. Exhibitions are even more expensive, costing anything upwards of £10K.

The web has introduced much more cost-effective ways to engage with customers, thereby offering a greater return on investment. This doesn't mean that businesses no longer need to attend exhibitions or have a sales team. However, they can use digital marketing *in conjunction with* some of the traditional methods — or, at least, those that are still around (Yellow Pages scrapped their print editions in 2017).

Wasted opportunities

Sadly, many businesses aren't taking advantage of these wonderful opportunities. Their websites receive few visitors and generate even fewer customers. To see why, let's explore the common traps businesses fall into when building their websites.

Trap 1: If it's cheap, you'll weep

In the past, any business wishing to market themselves would try to ensure that everything they produced was of a professional, high quality standard.

Then along came the internet and the notion that anyone, armed with a few simple software tools, could take care of their own online marketing at next to no cost. Appealing as this may sound, the results have rarely been anything but terrible.

I have seen businesses allow an inexperienced member of staff, with no long-term commitment, register a domain name and build a simple website only to give it up and disappear, leaving the business in the lurch. In extreme cases, unscrupulous web designers have held their clients to *ransom* for their own business domain name!

I urge you to think of your website as an important business asset and to treat it accordingly. Make sure your *company* owns both your domain and your website (as opposed to one individual who may one day leave). Also, make sure your website is hosted by a reliable, professional hosting company.

Trap 2: Build it and they will come

Do not think you can simply ignore digital marketing. Having a website without digital marketing is like setting up a store in a back alley and blacking out the windows! Nobody can find you or buy anything from you. Whatever kind of business you run — 'bricks and mortar', 'clicks and mortar' or 'full online business' — you need to have a comprehensive digital marketing strategy to support it.

Trap 3: I only need to do this once

Don't ignore what is happening online. The pace of change has been quite dramatic over the last ten years. Broadband adoption, tablets, smartphones, social media and Amazon have changed the way we think and operate. The attention deficit society, where people operate multiple devices at the same time, is here to stay. The next changes will probably include such things as more Artificial Intelligence, machine learning and virtual reality. Always keep abreast of what is happening in the digital world and how it can affect your business. If you don't, one of your competitors might!

The bottom line

- Understand the scope of digital marketing — and the amazing opportunities it presents.

- Take full advantage of these opportunities.

- Don't fall into the same common traps as some other companies!

CHAPTER 2: WEBSITE INSIGHT

Your website is only the start

Since you are reading this guide, I assume I don't need to convince you to have a website for your business. However, I *do* want to convince you to stop thinking of your website as your *complete* online presence. Your website is only a starting point — it may be the central hub of your digital marketing strategy, but it's far from sufficient on its own. I will expand on this point throughout the rest of this book.

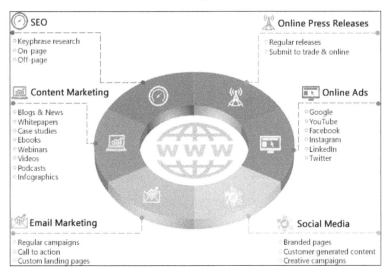

Figure 1: Digital marketing

Keeping your website up to date

You cannot simply build your website and then forget about it. You need to keep it up to date.

In the online world, everything is constantly evolving. Improvements in technology lead to changes in the style, appearance and functionality of websites. If you don't keep abreast of these changes, your website will soon start to look old and deliver a poor experience for your customers — driving them to your competitors.

Just to give you an idea, this is what the Amazon website looked like in 2002:

Welcome to Amazon.com Books!

One million titles, consistently low prices.

(If you explore just one thing, make it our personal notification service. We think it's very cool!)

SPOTLIGHT! -- AUGUST 16TH

These are the books we love, offered at Amazon.com low prices. The spotlight moves **EVERY** day so please come often.

ONE MILLION TITLES

Search Amazon.com's million title catalog by author, subject, title, keyword, and more... Or take a look at the books we recommend in over 20 categories... Check out our customer reviews and the award winners from the Hugo and Nebula to the Pulitzer and Nobel... and bestsellers are 30% off the publishers list...

EYES & EDITORS, A PERSONAL NOTIFICATION SERVICE

Like to know when that book you want comes out in paperback or when your favorite author releases a new title? Eyes, our tireless, automated search agent, will send you mail. Meanwhile, our human editors are busy previewing galleys and reading advance reviews. They can let you know when especially wonderful works are published in particular genres or subject areas. Come in, meet Eyes, and have it all explained.

YOUR ACCOUNT

Check the status of your orders or change the email address and password you have on file with us. Please note that you **do not** need an account to use the store. The first time you place an order, you will be given the opportunity to create an account.

Figure 2: Amazon website c 2000

And this is what it looked like a few years later in 2008:

Figure 3: Amazon website c 2008

Imagine what you would think if you went to Amazon today and it still looked like that! You would think they had fallen behind the times. It's the same when customers visit *your* site. If the majority of the sites your customers experience are easy to use, load quickly, work on both smartphones and desktops and look good, you have to make sure that your site keeps pace with the competition. As a general rule, plan to upgrade your site at least once every three years.

Here are some key events in the digital marketing world since 2003.

2000	Google's search engine gains traction
	Google launches AdWords
2002	Google launches Froogle
2003	Altavista loses its dominance as a search engine
	Altavista bought by Overture
	Overture bought by Yahoo!
	MySpace launches
	Google Florida algorithm update hits many businesses in the run-up to Christmas. The update penalises keyword stuffing.
	LinkedIn launches
2004	Google Austin update targets invisible test and meta-tag keyword stuffing
	Google Brandy update increases the importance of anchor text and link neighbourhoods
	Facebook launches
	Flickr launches
	Google search share hits 84.7%
	Firefox browser released
2005	YouTube launches
	Google Local Business Centre launches
	Google Jagger update attacks low-quality links (reciprocal, link farms and paid links)

	Google Big Daddy update tackles canonicalization and redirects
	Google launches Google Analytics following acquisition of Urchin
2006	Twitter launches
	Amazon AWS cloud services launch
	Facebook goes mobile
	Facebook opens to the world not just students
2007	First iPhone launches
	Google Universal search launches including news, video, images and local
	Microsoft Live Search replaces MSN search
2008	Google Chrome browser released
	Google introduces Suggest – a precursor to Google Instant
	Facebook hits 100 million users
2009	Google, Microsoft and Yahoo jointly announce canonical tag for indicating which URL to index
	Google real-time search launched shows news feeds real-time
	Facebook launches like button
	Bing replaces Microsoft's Live search
2010	The first iPad launched
	Instagram launches
	Pinterest launches

	Google Places page launched replacing Local Business Centre
	Google May Day updates its long-tail traffic indexing
	Google Caffeine update speeds up indexing and freshens the index
	Google instant previews of websites
	Google adjust algorithm to reduce rankings of businesses with bad reviews
	Google and Bing confirm they are using social signals
	Facebook hits 500 million users
	Microsoft takes over Yahoo! Search and runs ads under Microsoft adCentre
	Microsoft's Azure cloud platform launches
2011	Google Panda/Farmer update hits thin content and content farms. Additional releases of Panda roll out throughout the year
	Google, Yahoo and Microsoft support consolidated schema markup
	Google+ launches
	Google Freshness update looks for fresh content
	Apple's digital assistant Siri launched
2012	Google update demotes sites with ads above the fold
	Google Penguin update targets over-optimisation
	Google Knowledge Graph released showing additional information panels

	Facebook buys Instagram
	Facebook hits 1 billion users
	Google rebrands Froogle as Google Shopping
	Google launches BigQuery cloud platform
	Microsoft rebrands adCentre as Bing Ads
	Google DMCA penalty targets sites with repeat copyright violations
2013	Google Payday loan update targets payday land and porn sites
	Google In-depth articles results appear
	Google Hummingbird update focusses on conversational search yielding results where pages match the meaning to the query rather than just the words
2014	Google Panda 4.0 update targets press release sites
	Google Pigeon update aims at hyper-localising search results
	Google announces HTTPS as a ranking signal
	Apple Pay and Google Wallet launch
	Microsoft's digital assistant Cortana launched
2015	Facebook hits 1.5 billion users
	Google launches Google Certified Shops for UK e-commerce merchants
	Google mobile-friendly update favours mobile friendly websites
	Google restructures under Alphabet umbrella

	AOL takes over Bing ads and replaces Google's results with Bing's on AOL properties
	Google local search results listings reduced to 3
2016	Google removes ads from right-hand side
	Google Accelerated Mobile Pages for publishers
	Amazon launches Echo in the UK
	Amazon launches Dash button in the UK
	Google boosts mobile-friendly ranking signal
2017	Facebook hits 2 billion users
	Google site search to shut down
	Google assistant launched

Types of change

The online world is one of constant change and evolution — and sometimes things can change with startling rapidity. Here are some of the different *types* of change that you need to take into account when updating your online presence.

Technology

Internet technology is evolving all the time. Every year, there are new things that websites can do that simply weren't possible before.

For example, the devices that people are using multiply and evolve all the time. Once upon a time, you only needed to make sure your website looked good on desktop PCs (and even then, you had to pick a display resolution you thought most people used). Today, it's unthinkable to have a site that doesn't work well on mobile devices.

You need to keep pace with these and other technological changes and understand how they impact your online presence and trade.

Search engine algorithms

I have devoted a whole chapter of this book to 'search engine optimisation' (SEO), which basically means making sure customers can find you online. However, the people who run Google and other search engines are constantly changing how they index and search websites — their 'search algorithms'.

You have to make sure you keep up to date with these changes and that your site satisfies the latest requirements. In 2016, for example, Google changed its algorithm to favour mobile-responsive sites and reinforced its commitment to secure websites. If you don't already have a secure, mobile-responsive site, then you need to correct this as a matter of urgency. It's important to stay on top of how the various search engines work and adapt your strategy to take advantage of relevant changes.

Economic and legal

Cyber crime is a sad fact of modern life and has led to an increased emphasis on privacy and making sure customer data is processed securely. It's important that your website is secure and complies with all current legal requirements. For example, the Companies Act requires you to state your registered company number on your website as well as your principal registered office.

You also have to pay attention to Privacy and Electronic Communications Regulations and the EU General Data Protection Regulation.

At the time of writing this book, UK company websites are subject to relevant EU regulations. The Brexit negotiations will obviously have some effect on this. It's important to keep on top of these fluctuating legal requirements.

Content management systems

So, you understand the need to keep your website up to date. What's the best way to do this?

A content management system (CMS) can help you a great deal. A CMS allows you to create, edit and remove content from a website without having *any* technical knowledge. The arrival of various CMS options was a wonderful step in the history of the web as it enables you to update your website quickly, without relying on a programmer or designer and without learning any computer code. Having a good CMS is vital for strong customer engagement and adding new search-engine indexable content to your site.

When building a new website, you need to consider which content management system to use.

I see an increasing number of businesses using Wordpress, which started as a fairly simple blogging platform but is now the basis for some 75 million websites all over the world. It is what's known as an 'open source' platform, meaning there's no single 'owner' dictating how it evolves and improves. Instead, there's an entire community of Wordpress users who contribute to its ongoing development, such as devising new 'plugins' and 'widgets' (specialised bits of software that add extra functionality to your website). This means you can build a pretty good website relatively quickly and at low cost. If all you need is a simple 'brochure' website, including a 'call to action' to generate leads, then Wordpress can be an excellent solution.

However, Wordpress has two significant disadvantages:

- Security.
- Speed.

Because Wordpress is an open source platform, and very widely used, it tends to be targeted by spam and scam artists. You *can* keep a Wordpress site safe and secure from attack, but it's not easy and requires constant vigilance. Make sure you follow the recommended security best practices for Wordpress and install Wordfence, or similar software, to protect against attack.

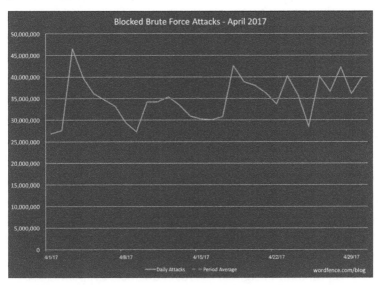

Figure 4: Brute force attacks on WordPress April 2017

The second problem is that many Wordpress sites are slow and not as responsive as they should be. The fact that it's an open source platform means it's fairly easy for you to modify your site, change some of the templates, add new functions and so on. However, unless you're careful and know what you're doing, making these kinds of changes can leave you with a website that performs rather slowly from the user's point of view. This is obviously bad news since it can drive potential customers away. Another problem is that your website's speed, and how responsive it is, affects your Google ranking. If your site is rather slow, you'll end up lower down the search engine results pages. This is not an insurmountable issue. You can work with a good web development agency to make sure your Wordpress site is well designed and highly responsive.

As I have said, Wordpress is an excellent platform in many ways. However, if you are going to build a commercial website — especially one that gathers customer data — you have to consider whether the security issues associated with Wordpress are going to be a problem. You may decide to consider other platforms instead.

Your website budget

One of the first things our clients want to know is how much a website costs. The sad thing is that they rarely ask how much their digital marketing budget should be. Here's a rule of thumb — you should be spending 7-12% of your annual turnover on marketing. On average, businesses spend 35% of their marketing budget on *digital* marketing (including their website). This figure is (or should be) even higher If you are running a wholly online business.

Of course, there are many factors to take into consideration, such as your gross margin and the intensity of your competition.

The bottom line

- Your website is a fundamental asset of your business.

- Keep up to date with design, technology, search engine, economic and legal changes.

- Make sure you update your website in line with technology, search engine and design trends and legal changes.

CHAPTER 3: CYBER SECURITY AND DATA PROTECTION

Threat and defence

One of the biggest threats businesses face today is cyber attack — unauthorised people 'hacking' into your system and causing problems (such as stealing data, posting unauthorised content or even taking your entire site down). This book is about digital marketing, not data protection, so I won't go into all the complexities of how to defend yourself against these kinds of attacks. What I will say is that you *must* ensure that your website is protected against attack. What's more, if your site *is* attacked, you need to know how to limit the damage and recover from it quickly. If your website is down due to cyber attack, your customers will forgive you... at first. After a while, if you don't seem to be fixing the problem, they will simply move to your competitors.

Make sure you:

- Build a good website with the right level of security for your business.

- Host with a reliable hosting company.

- Ensure the hosting company is ISO 27001 certified (the international standard that covers information security).

- Ensure your hosting company provides the required level of security.

- Understand your hosting company's recovery process for attacks or technical failures.

- Consider anti-malware and intrusion detection systems suitable for the type of website you operate.

- If you run an e-commerce site, understand the Payment Card Industry Data Security Standard (PCI DSS) requirements and make sure that you are compliant.

General Data Protection Regulation (GDPR)

The EU General Data Protection Regulation (GDPR) came into force on 25 May 2018.

The GDPR supersedes the UK Data Protection Act 1998. It expands the rights of individuals to control how their personal information is collected and processed, and places new obligations on organisations regarding data protection. Organisations in breach of the GDPR face penalties of up to 4% of annual global turnover or €20 million, whichever is greater. It's clear that GDPR is not to be taken lightly.

The difference between EU regulations and directives

EU legislation can be divided into directives and regulations.

- **Directives** set out common goals that EU member states must enact into their own laws.

- **Regulations** on the other hand are binding laws that apply directly in member states and require no domestic law to enact them. The EU ePrivacy Regulation (ePR) and the GDPR fall under this category.

The Data Protection Act was based on a *directive*, which is why compliance across the EU was so variable. The GDPR has to be implemented as written (although some member states may be exempt in certain areas).

In order to comply with GDPR, you must be able to demonstrate compliance with six data protection principles. This involves adopting safe data protection policies, ensuring appropriate procedures are in place to deal with the provisions of the regulation and building a workplace culture of data privacy and security.

As a business owner, you may be shuddering at the prospect of GDPR compliance. However, you should think of it as something that will enhance your reputation with your customers, not just a set of penalties to avoid.

Personal data

The GDPR applies to personal data. This means any information that can directly or indirectly identify a person, regardless of the format used. Personal data includes someone's name, address, email address, photograph, IP address, location, online behaviour (usually tracked using cookies), profiling and analytics data.

In addition, the GDPR introduced stringent controls on specific categories of personal data: race, religion, political opinions, trade union membership, sexual orientation, health information and biometric and genetic data. The inclusion of biometric and genetic data is new.

Scope

The GDPR applies to all EU organisations — commercial businesses, charities or public authorities — that collect, store or process the personal data of individuals residing in the EU (even if they're not EU citizens).

Organisations outside the EU that sell goods or services to anyone within the EU, paid or unpaid, are also subject to the GDPR.

Any organisation is the data controller regarding any personal data for which it determines the means and purposes of processing. A third party (such as a service provider) that processes data on behalf of a controller will have new legally defined obligations and becomes a data processor. These include the requirement to only process data in accordance with a contract with each controller.

Your website hosting provider and email marketing service (or marketing automation provider) are all examples of data processors under the GDPR.

Joint controllers share the obligations. If you agree with a partner to host a webinar and share the leads, then you also share the controller obligations in respect of any personal data involved.

Data protection principles and practices

At the heart of GDPR are six principles governing the protection of personal data. It must be:

- Processed lawfully, fairly and transparently.
- Collected only for specific legitimate purposes.
- Limited to what is relevant and necessary.
- Accurate and kept up to date.
- Stored only as long as is necessary.
- Protected by appropriate measures concerning security, integrity and confidentiality.

Accountability and governance

To demonstrate GDPR compliance, you must be able to show the following:

- The establishment of a governance structure with roles and responsibilities for personal data protection — which almost certainly means that company directors must be actively involved.

- Detailed records of all data processing operations.

- Documentation of data protection policies and procedures.

- Data protection impact assessments (DPIAs) for high-risk processing operations.

- The implementation of appropriate measures to secure personal data.

- Staff training and awareness regarding data security.

- (In some cases) the appointment of a data protection officer.

Data protection by design and by default

You need to consider effective data protection practices and safeguards *before* you start processing any personal, sensitive or important data. This means that whenever you build a website, or undertake any digital marketing, you work out detailed data protection policies from the outset.

- Consider data protection at the *design* stage of any new process, system or technology.

- Conduct a Data Protection Impact Assessment (DPIA) as an integral part of your data protection policies.

- Your default policy must always be to collect only the personal data that is absolutely necessary for a specific purpose.

Lawful processing

You must identify and document the lawful basis for any processing of personal data, which must be one of the following:

- You have consent from the individual.
- The data is needed to perform a contract.
- You are protecting the vital interests of the individual.
- It is needed to fulfil the legal obligations of the organisation.
- It is in the public interest to process the data.
- It is within the legitimate interests of the organisation.

Many businesses assume that lawful processing of personal data *always* requires direct consent from the individual. This is not necessarily so. For example, if you are running an e-commerce business you have to obtain some personal information in order to fulfil the contract you have with each customer. This contractual requirement would be the basis for your lawful processing of personal data, not direct consent.

Valid consent

There are strict rules for obtaining consent:

- Consent must be freely given, specific, informed and unambiguous.

- A request for consent must be intelligible and in clear, plain language.

- Passive opt-in (such as pre-ticked forms) and opt-in by default will no longer constitute 'consent'.

- Customers must be able to withdraw consent at any time.

- Consent for online services from anyone under 13 is only valid with parental authorisation.

- You must be able to show evidence of consent if required.

The new legislation also requires 'granular' consent policies — meaning that you can't rely on one indication of consent to cover everything you do. For example, suppose a customer consents to receive emails from you. If you also want to share their data with a third party, the customer has to consent to this separately.

Privacy rights of individuals

The GDPR enhances and extends an individuals' rights in a number of important areas:

- The right of access to personal data through subject access requests.

- The right to correct inaccurate personal data.

- The right in certain cases to have personal data erased.

- The right to object to such things as 'processing based on legitimate interests' and 'processing for the purposes of historical research'.

- The right to move personal data from one service provider to another (data portability).

Transparency and privacy notices

Organisations must be clear and transparent about how personal data is going to be processed, by whom and why. Privacy notices must be provided in a concise, transparent and easily accessible form, using clear and plain language.

Data transfers outside the EU

The transfer of personal data outside the EU is only allowed:

- Where the EU has designated the country receiving the data as providing an adequate level of data protection.
- Through model contracts or binding corporate rules.
- By complying with an approved certification mechanism, e.g. EU-US Privacy Shield.

Many cloud service providers store or process personal data outside the EU. This is illegal under the GDPR unless permitted for one of the three reasons stated above. This is also the case under the current Data Protection Act, but the GDPR introduces much more severe penalties for non-compliance.

Data security and breach reporting

To comply with GDPR, you need to ensure that all personal data is secured against both unauthorised processing and accidental loss, destruction or damage.

- You must report data breaches to the relevant data protection authority within 72 hours of discovery.
- You must notify affected individuals if there is a significant risk to their rights and freedoms, e.g. identity theft and personal safety.

You don't need to contact individuals if you have appropriate protective measures in place to ensure they will never be in any personal danger — such as making sure their data is securely encrypted. It is also advisable to encrypt the *transmission* of data. Unfortunately, there is no current certification or badged scheme for GDPR compliance but I expect this will change in future. However, when you are choosing or working with hosting providers, you should at least insist on ISO 27001 certification. This pertains to data security and will aid your case if ever you need to prove GDPR compliance.

The role of the data protection officer (DPO)

The appointment of a DPO is mandatory for:

- Public authorities.

- Organisations involved in high-risk data processing.

- Organisations processing special categories of data.

A DPO is a protected role and has specific responsibilities, including:

- To Inform and advise the organisation of its obligations under the GDPR.

- To monitor compliance, including training staff appropriately, raising awareness about data security throughout the organisation and conducting data audits.

- To cooperate with data protection authorities and act as a contact point.

Practical examples

© marketoonist.com

You may feel that GDPR requirements seem rather intimidating at first. Before you run off screaming, let's look at some practical examples of how the GDPR works *for* your business and actually helps your digital marketing.

Websites

If you run an e-commerce website, you will be collecting personal information for accounting and order fulfilment purposes. The need to fulfil the contract gives you a lawful basis for collecting personal data. Your privacy policy should state this.

For lead generation websites, you will be collecting information in order to provide respondents with further information. In this case, the lawful basis for collecting personal data is the customer's consent to provide further information. Your privacy policy should state this.

In both cases (e-commerce and lead generation) you should be able to delete a visitor's personal data if requested and provided there's no legal requirement to retain that data. For example, you may need to retain a record of a transaction for accounting and tax purposes.

Your site should also allow you to download a visitor's data to send to that visitor if they ask for it.

Whichever kind of website you maintain, you will almost invariably have Google Analytics installed to track the behaviour of people who visit the site (which pages they click on, and so on). Google is therefore the Data Controller. You cannot identify any individual visitor to your site from Google Analytics as it only gathers purely statistical data. However, you need to state in your cookie policy that you use Google Analytics to track and analyse the performance of your website.

The same applies if you install any other tracking software, such as Hotjar.

If you remarket through Google, Facebook or any other platform, based on visits to your site, you need to update your privacy policy to state this.

You also need to avoid hosting your website outside the EU unless the hosting country complies with the cross-border mechanisms allowed by the GDPR. An example would be the EU-US Privacy Shield. This allows you to have your site hosted in the USA provided the hosting company is registered with the Privacy Shield and has either a physical presence or a representative in the EU.

Email marketing

For email marketing, you are entitled to harvest email addresses based on either consent or legitimate business interest. For example, suppose a customer buys a product from you. If you send that customer emails about that product or other products in the same range, this is allowed. However, you must always provide an opt-out mechanism.

You are allowed to use dynamic personalisation, provided the customer consents or if the content you display is directly relevant to the customer's previous purchases. (Dynamic personalisation means the displayed content is personalised, based on the customer's previous choices or behaviour).

Paid advertising

You can advertise via Google, Bing, Facebook, LinkedIn or Twitter without any worries. It's up to these sites and companies that carry the advertising to make sure they are GDPR compliant.

However, this is only the case for simple 'search and display' advertising. As soon as you use remarketing and custom audience targeting you either need the customer's consent or a lawful basis for doing so. It is most likely that you will require consent and you should update your website privacy policy to make this clear.

Social media marketing

Whichever social media platforms you use, they will have to ensure that they are GDPR compliant.

Marketing automation

Most marketing automation platforms record visitor IPs and other information. (An Internet Protocol or 'IP' address is a unique number that identifies a device connected to the internet. The GDPR regards IP addresses as personally identifiable information.)

Your privacy policy must make it clear that you are doing this on the basis of 'legitimate interest'. The logic here is that if someone is visiting your site they are expressing an interest in your products and services.

Once you get beyond basic IP tracking, you would probably want to capture the visitor's email address. To do this, you either need the visitor's consent or an alternative legal basis for processing their data. This being the case, you would need to update your privacy policy accordingly. You would have to give the visitor the right to ask for their data to be removed and to have their data transferred to them if they ask for it.

Most marketing automation platforms are cloud-based. Make sure that if your platform is hosted in the USA that it is registered with the EU-US Privacy Shield and that they have an office or representative in the EU.

What next?

If you haven't already done so, you need to:

- Conduct a data inventory and data flow audit to identify what personal data you hold, who you have shared it with and where and how it is stored.

- Review existing processes for gathering personal data and determine the business and lawful justifications for these processes.

- Ensure these processes comply with the GDPR.

- Identify where the data resides physically. If you are hosting on a cloud platform ensure that either it is based within the EU or that the hosting company is GDPR compliant. You also need to make sure you have a legal basis for the trans-border processing.

- Document your GDPR compliance. As a data controller, you are likely to be outsourcing some activities (e.g. hosting and email marketing). You must obtain assurances from any companies that handle data on your behalf that they are GDPR compliant and have the appropriate documentation to prove it if required.

- Secure supplier relationships by reviewing your contracts with third parties in line with GDPR requirements.[1]

Privacy and Electronic Communications Regulations (PECR) and EU ePrivacy Regulation (ePR)

The Privacy and Electronic Communications Regulations (PECR) currently govern the following:

- Marketing by electronic means.

---

1 Calder, A. (n.d.). EU GDPR A Pocket Guide. In A. Calder, *EU GDPR A Pocket Guide.* ITGP.

- The use of cookies to track information about people visiting a website.

- Security of electronic services.

- Privacy of customers using electronic communication networks.

In this section, I will simply cover the requirements for email marketing and cookie notices as these are relevant to digital marketing. I will not cover telephone or fax marketing, or the rules for organisations that provide networks or electronic service providers. (Does anyone still do fax marketing? We no longer have a fax machine at Xanthos!)

The PECR for email marketing are essentially about protecting the personal information of individuals held and used by organisations.

The PECR specifies that you cannot send marketing emails to individuals without their specific consent. Your current customers can be deemed to have a 'soft opt-in', which simply means that because they bought from you before they are happy to receive marketing emails from you. However, you must provide a way for them to opt-out both at the time of their first purchase and every time you email them. You can also send marketing emails to companies but, again, you must provide an opt-out option.

You can buy and use email marketing lists so long as whoever compiled the list obtained consent from everyone on it. I don't advise using purchased lists as they have a lower engagement rate than your own nurtured list.

While the PECR allows for marketing to companies, the GDPR deems an individual's work email address to be personal data.

Cookie notices are covered by the PECR. A cookie is a small text file that is automatically downloaded from your website to each visitor's device. It allows you to store some information about the visitor and their preferences. The PECR requires you to explain clearly to each visitor that your site uses cookies. You also have to say why you use them and what they do. You also need to get the visitor's consent to your use of cookies. The simple way to do this is to add a small notice to your website asking each visitor to acknowledge and accept the use of cookies.

You can read the relevant regulations on the ICO's website:

https://ico.org.uk/for-organisations/guide-to-pecr/introduction/what-are-pecr/

What is the ePR?

In 2003, the European Commission published the PECR (Privacy and Electronic Communications Regulations). In 2017, as part of a new strategy regarding the digital single market, a new regulation was created called ePR. This has not yet replaced PECR, but it will do so eventually.

Although it addresses more or less the same concerns as the PECR, this new regulation has broader scope. It aims to create more robust privacy across *all* electronic communications. For example, it addresses privacy issues arising from 'machine-to-machine' communications, which the PECR did not. This is important in the era of what is often referred to as 'the Internet of Things (IoT)'.

The territorial reach of the ePR is the same as for the GDPR. Wherever GDPR applies, ePR does too. They even share the same penalties for failure to comply. The original plan was for ePR to come into effect at the same time as GDPR (25

May 2018). However, this didn't happen and it might not be introduced much before May 2019.

As and when the ePR *is* finally introduced, it will bring with it quite a few changes. For example, it will be possible to use 'cookies' without requiring the end-user to agree. The idea is that more sophisticated browser settings will govern how user information is collected and shared. As a result, we should see fewer banners notifying users about cookies.

Within the UK, enforcement of the ePR is, or will be, the responsibility of the Information Commissioner's Office (ICO). When the ePR comes into effect, the ICO will issue guidelines regarding compliance.

The ePR and the GDPR

In the UK, the GDPR will be enacted by the new Data Protection Bill. The GDPR concerns the processing of personal data. The ePR has been designed to complement it by providing specific rules "regarding the protection of fundamental rights and freedoms of natural and legal persons in the provision and use of electronic communications services".

What does this mean in practice?

Firstly, make sure you check the law when it is finalised as it is entirely possible it will be pared back. Secondly, there is a view that the GDPR means B2B email marketing will have to follow the same rules as B2C. You used to be able to send B2B emails with impunity so long as you provided a way to opt out. Now you will have to obtain prior consent or some other lawful basis to send marketing emails to a B2B address, just as you do for B2C emails.

The bottom line

- One of the biggest threats businesses face today is cyber attack. Make sure you defend your business and website against these kinds of attacks.

- See cyber security as a good thing, that works *for* you, not an onerous chore.

- Make sure you understand GDPR and that you implement all the necessary policies and procedures to be GDPR compliant.

- Build data protection by design and by default into all your website development and digital marketing processes.

- Understand the requirements of both the PECR and the new ePR when they come into effect, and comply with them.

CHAPTER 4: DIGITAL MARKETING STRATEGY

Creating a DM strategy

Many businesses have a clearly defined business plan. Far fewer businesses have a digital marketing strategy, which makes it more or less impossible to succeed in today's world. Whatever your business strategy, you *also* need a digital marketing strategy.

At Xanthos we like to keep the creation of a digital marketing strategy straightforward. Here is our 7-step digital marketing strategy for SMEs:

1. Define your market. You have probably already done this as part of defining your business strategy, but you need to analyse your *online* market. First of all, you need to research the demand for your products or services to understand your online market. You need to understand the types of questions your target customers are asking online and find the most popular content relevant to your business. You also need to understand the key influencers in your market.

2. Conduct a SWOT analysis (strengths, weaknesses, opportunities, threats). You have probably done this as part of your overall business strategy, but you need to apply the same analysis to your digital marketing. We suggest you treat strengths and weaknesses as *internal* and opportunities and threats as *external*. It's important to analyse what your online competitors are doing. Check how successful they are in terms of SEO, traffic and conversion, content, use of social media and digital marketing.

3. Define your target audience. Start with a top-level definition of your target audience. Next, go into greater detail to define one or more target personas — an example of the sort of person you are trying to reach. This helps to focus your marketing efforts. To define a persona, you need to cover:

   a. Their background: education, work experience and marital status.

   b. Demographics: typical age and income bracket.

   c. Description: demeanour, mannerisms, buzz words, tone and style preferences and which media or online channels they are likely to use.

   d. Goals: what is this hypothetical person's top two goals?

   e. Challenges: what are this person's main challenges? What problems do they want or need to solve?

   f. How do you help this person? How do you solve their challenges and help them achieve their goals?

   g. Quotes: get quotes about their goals and challenges from *real* people (such as current customers) who closely match your hypothetical person.

   h. Objections: the most common objections your persona is likely to raise during the sales process.

   i. Marketing message: decide how you will present your solution to your target persona.

j. Elevator pitch: reduce what you want to say to this persona to a short, simple message you use consistently throughout your company.

4. Define your USP (unique selling proposition) or, alternatively, your value proposition. You need one or the other if you want to successfully market your products or services against the competition. Crafting your USP is one of the hardest things to do. You are really answering the question, "Why should prospective buyers, who meet your ideal customer profile, buy your product/service from you rather than your competitors?" If you can, create a USP that has three elements: it is specific, quantified and verified. This works better than only having one or two of these elements.

5. The three Ps. Define your product, pricing and positioning (often referred to as place).

6. The fourth P: Promotion. When you define your digital marketing strategy, you need to consider the different channels available to you. This usually involves considering both 'inbound' and 'outbound' marketing. Inbound marketing is about using content to attract potential customers to your business. Outbound marketing is the more traditional practice of getting your message to customers (even if they haven't asked for it). Cold calling, direct mail and advertising are all examples of outbound marketing. Digital marketing can include both inbound and outbound strategies. At Xanthos, we tend to use a combination of both for our clients. Define how you will promote your products or services. In the context of digital marketing, you would typically include:

a. SEO.

b. PR.

c. Content marketing.

d. Social media marketing.

e. Email marketing.

f. Paid advertising.

7. Plan. Once you have devised your strategy, you need to put a plan together for the year ahead. In simple terms, you state who will do what by when, including targets — these give you a way to measure your performance against the plan.

That's the complete 7-step digital marketing strategy. Once you have your strategy in place, you have to put it into action. You need the human resources and budget to deliver the plan. Make sure you review your performance monthly and make adjustments where necessary.

You can use this template to create your digital marketing strategy.

Market
What market are you in?
SWOT
What are your internal strengths?

What are your internal weaknesses?
What are your external opportunities?
What are your external threats?
Target audience
What is your product(s)/service(s)?
Who will buy these products/services?
How many personas are you targeting (normally you would have 1 or 2)?

Complete a persona profile for each target persona

USP

Why would your target persona buy from you rather than your competition?

3Ps

Describe your products/services?

How are you going to price your products/services?

What is your positioning of your products/services in your market? How do you want your customers to view your products/services?

4th P Promotion
How will you market your products online?
• SEO
• PR
• Content marketing
• Social media marketing

• Email marketing
• Paid advertising
Plan
Create detailed plan – see the following example

Digital marketing plan example

What	Who	Frequency	KPIs
Search engine optimisation			Ranking Trust flow Citation flow Organic traffic Conversion rate Return on investment
- Research terms		Initial and annual	
- On page optimisation		Initial and for each new page	
- Title and description tags		Initial and for each new page	
- Incoming links		X per month	Number of backlinks
- Sitemaps		Initial and dynamic feed	
- Local		Initial and annual review	
Press releases		Create quarterly PR calendar	
		x per month or per quarter	Reach Interactions

4: Digital marketing strategy

What	Who	Frequency	KPIs
Content marketing		Create quarterly content calendar	
- Blog posts		X per week/per month	# of blog subscribers Blog traffic
- Whitepapers		X per month/per quarter	X downloads per week/month
- Ebooks		X per quarter/per year	X downloads per week/month
- Videos		X per quarter /per year	X views per week/month
- Infographics		X per quarter/per year	
Social media marketing		Create social media calendar	
- Twitter		X posts per day	# of followers # of likes # of retweets # of comments Traffic from Twitter Conversion rate
- Facebook		X posts per day	# of followers # of likes # of shares

What	Who	Frequency	KPIs
			# of comments Traffic from Facebook Conversion rate
- LinkedIn		X posts per day	# of followers # of likes # of shares # of comments Traffic from LinkedIn Conversion rate
- Instagram		X posts per day	# of followers # of likes # of comments Traffic from Instagram Conversion rate
- YouTube		X videos per quarter/per year	# of video views # of subscribers # of likes # of comments Traffic from YouTube

What	Who	Frequency	KPIs
			Conversion rate
Email Marketing		Create quarterly calendar	
		X campaigns per month	# of email subscribers Open rate Click-through rate Conversion rate
Paid Advertising			
- Google AdWords		Search, display, remarketing, shopping ads setup. Daily/weekly management	Click-through rate Conversion rate Cost per acquisition Return on ad spend
- Bing Ads		Search, display, remarketing, shopping ads setup. Daily/weekly management	Click-through rate Conversion rate Cost per acquisition Return on ad spend
- Facebook Ads		Engagement campaign Product campaign Daily/weekly management	Click-through rate Conversion rate Cost per acquisition

What	Who	Frequency	KPIs
			Return on ad spend

The bottom line

- Set out your 7-step digital marketing strategy.
- Complete your digital marketing plan.
- Measure performance monthly.

CHAPTER 5: SEARCH ENGINE OPTIMISATION (SEO)

In search of higher rankings

You may already have heard about search engine optimisation (SEO). However, just for completeness, let me explain what it is and how it has evolved.

Google displays results differently depending on the search term, time, location, personalisation and other factors.

Let's look at the search results for the term 'omega', as shown in Figure 5.

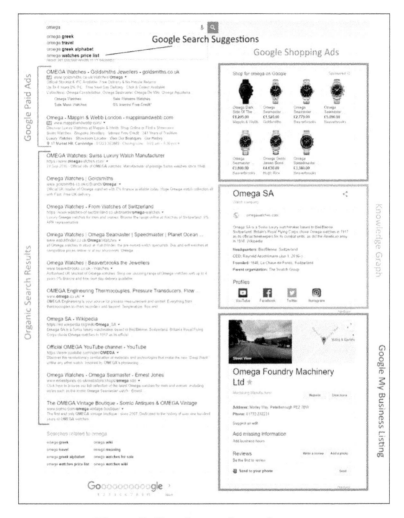

Figure 5: Google search results page

Organic (or natural listings) are unpaid search results. You cannot pay to rank in these listings.

SEO is the optimisation of websites for the specific purpose of getting your website to rank high on search engines results pages (SERPs).

In the UK today the top 5 search engines are:

- Google
- Bing
- Yahoo!
- MSN
- DuckDuckGo

However, the market share of these search engines differs dramatically, as shown in Figure 6.

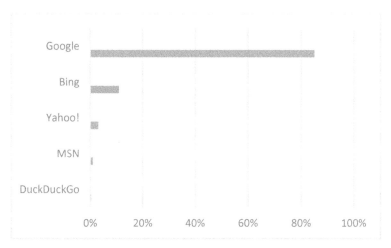

Figure 6: Search engine market share in the UK
Source: Statista, 2018

Given Google's dominant market share, I will focus on Google for the rest of this section.

The higher your Google ranking, the more likely it is that people will click on your listing to get to your website.

Ideally, you want to get in the top three places on SERPs, because these get about 63% of all the clicks for any given search term (based on statistics from May 2018).

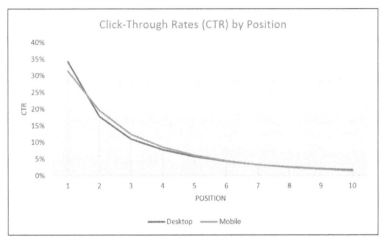

Figure 7: Source: AWR
https://www.advancedwebranking.com/cloud/ctrstudy/

Clearly, you want to achieve one of the top three positions if you possibly can. Getting featured on the second page of Google search results isn't worth a whole lot. The only time I've seen a second-page listing work is when Google's algorithm, rather uncharacteristically, doesn't yield the results that people are looking for on the first page.

AWR (who provided the graph above) also collect data regarding the click-through rate for branded versus non-branded search terms. Not surprisingly, the click-through rate for branded terms, for the top three search results, increases from 63% to nearer 75%.

Long tail terms

Another interesting factor is the impact of 'long tail' terms. A one-word search term generally has a lower click-through rate than a two-, three- or four-word search term. One-word terms achieve roughly a 45% click-through rate in the top three positions while a four-word term achieves closer to a 70% click-through rate.

An example would be someone searching for "solicitor" versus "solicitor conveyancing" versus "solicitor conveyancing Cambridge". A one-word term gives no indication of the intent of the searcher — they may just be looking for general information or even the definition of a word. If you are a firm of solicitors that specialise in certain areas, getting a good Google ranking for a one-word search term like 'solicitor' is likely to be costly without attracting many of the clients you want. On the other hand, if you aim to achieve a high ranking for the more precise term 'solicitor conveyancing Cambridge', you are likely to attract far more relevant traffic to your site.

This is the result for a one-word search term:

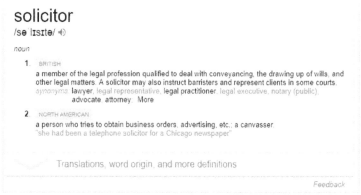

Figure 8: Google search results for "solicitor"

5: Search engine optimisation (SEO)

You can see that Google assumes the searcher is looking for a definition. It follows this with a Map listing of three solicitor's firms, the Law Society's website, the Wikipedia listing for 'solicitor' and a student job site!

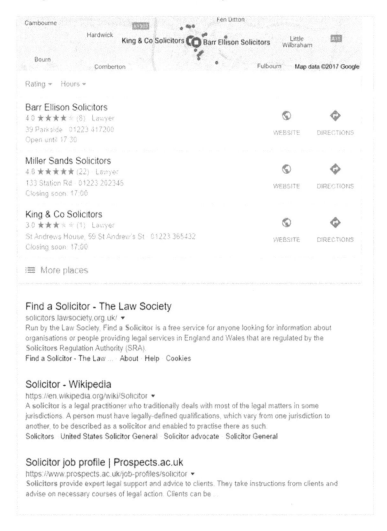

Rating ▾   Hours ▾

Barr Ellison Solicitors
4 0 ★★★★☆ (8)   Lawyer
39 Parkside   01223 417200
Open until 17 30
                                    WEBSITE   DIRECTIONS

Miller Sands Solicitors
4 8 ★★★★★ (22)   Lawyer
133 Station Rd   01223 202345
Closing soon 17:00
                                    WEBSITE   DIRECTIONS

King & Co Solicitors
3 0 ★★★☆☆ (1)   Lawyer
St Andrews House, 59 St Andrew's St 01223 365432
Closing soon 17:00
                                    WEBSITE   DIRECTIONS

≡ More places

Find a Solicitor - The Law Society
solicitors.lawsociety.org.uk/ ▾
Run by the Law Society, Find a Solicitor is a free service for anyone looking for information about organisations or people providing legal services in England and Wales that are regulated by the Solicitors Regulation Authority (SRA).
Find a Solicitor - The Law ... About Help Cookies

Solicitor - Wikipedia
https://en.wikipedia.org/wiki/Solicitor ▾
A solicitor is a legal practitioner who traditionally deals with most of the legal matters in some jurisdictions. A person must have legally-defined qualifications, which vary from one jurisdiction to another, to be described as a solicitor and enabled to practise there as such.
Solicitors United States Solicitor General Solicitor advocate Solicitor General

Solicitor job profile | Prospects.ac.uk
https://www.prospects.ac.uk/job-profiles/solicitor ▾
Solicitors provide expert legal support and advice to clients. They take instructions from clients and advise on necessary courses of legal action. Clients can be ...

Here are the 'related searches' that Google suggests for the term 'solicitor':

Searches related to solicitor

solicitors meaning	solicitor **salary**
solicitor **near me**	solicitor **job description**
solicitor **vs barrister**	solicitor **fees**
solicitor **conveyancing**	solicitor **meaning in hindi**

Figure 9: Google search suggestions for solicitor

By way of contrast, if you search using the three-word term 'solicitor conveyancing Cambridge', the result looks like those shown in Figure 10.

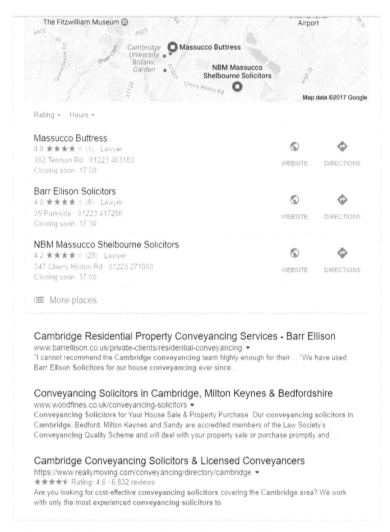

Figure 10: Google search results for solicitor conveyancing Cambridge

After the map listings, the first two results are for solicitors that offer conveyancing services.

Whether you try to optimise your Google ranking based on one, two, three or four-word search terms will depend on your market and what you are trying to achieve.

In our solicitor example, if you want to educate potential clients about what a solicitor does then the results for a one-word search term are fine. However, if you want to focus on lead generation for a particular service, trying to achieve a high ranking for a long tail keyword would be a better strategy.

How do you get a high ranking?

At Xanthos, we often get asked to achieve a 'top three' Google ranking for a client's website. Here is the key question you have to ask yourself:

"Why would Google rank your website number one for your given search terms?"

If you can answer this question comprehensively then you probably don't need to do anything else — you have already done enough to secure the top Google ranking!

You will get a high ranking if your answer includes all the following:

1. You have 'killer' content on your website (relevant to your chosen search terms).

2. Your killer content has attracted excellent incoming links from authoritative sites.

3. Your site provides fresh new content on the subject matter.

4. You have a well-built website: the code is clean, the site is fast, secure and mobile responsive, and all the right markup is in place.

5. You have written the right title tags for your content and descriptions.

6. You don't spam keywords or links.

Where to start

Keyphrase analysis

The first thing to do is find out what terms your customers are using to search for your products and/or services. *Warning: do not assume you know!*

Many businesses make the mistake of *assuming* they know which terms their customers are using when they search online. To see how this can go badly wrong, consider companies that lend money. In the early days of the internet, lenders assumed that their target market used the search term 'lending'. What they eventually discovered was that, in fact, they used the term 'borrowing' — a small but crucial difference!

Start with the search terms you *think* your target audience might use and research them. There are four main tools that will help you to do this:

- Google Keyword Planner.
- Google Trends.
- Google Search Console.
- Google Search Suggestions.

The Google Keyword Planner allows you to try out different search terms and see (a) how many people tap those words into Google (known as the 'search volume'), and (b) how many other businesses are currently trying to attract people based on those terms. Ideally, you want to choose search terms that combine high search volume with low competition.

You will need to set up a Google AdWords account to access the Keyword Planner. Here is the link to the planner:

https://adwords.google.com/intl/en_uk/home/tools/keyword -planner/

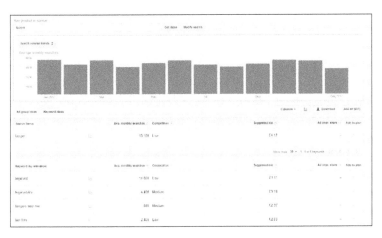

Figure 11: Example using Keyword Planner

The Google Trends report will give you the trend for a particular search term over a period of time. You can specify the location and time that interests you. You can access Google Trends here: *https://trends.google.com/trends/.*

Figure 12: Example using Google Trends

When you type a particular search term into Google, related terms appear in the dropdown menu and at the foot of the page.

Figure 13: Example of search suggestion

Google Search Console

The Google Search Console provides a wealth of information about your website, from its 'indexing health' to what are known as 'crawl errors'. If you have an established website, the Search Console tells you which search terms people are using to find it.

The term 'organic' is used to refer to all the search results *other* than adverts and sponsored links. You can link your Search Console with your Google Analytics account to see organic search information:

https://www.google.com/webmasters/tools/

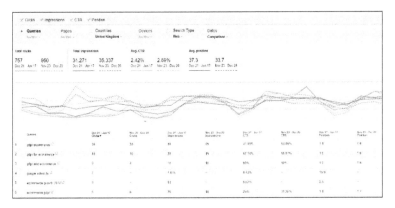

Figure 14: Example of Google Search Console search queries

On-page optimisation

Once you have identified which search terms you want to use to attract customers, you need to optimise the pages of your website accordingly. Here is a list of top-level on-page factors you need to address:

- Title tag.
- Meta description tag.
- H1 tags.
- Images.
- Content.
- Domain name.

- Architecture.

- Robots.txt.

- XML sitemaps.

- 301 redirects.

Title tags

Title tags tell search engines, and potential customers, what your page is about. Always include your target search terms. The title tag sits within the source code of your page. If you are using a good content management system, you should be able to write your title tag in the designated field.

It is important that you write a unique title tag for each page on your website. *Never* duplicate a title tag across two or more pages.

The optimum length for a title tag has changed over the years, so always be sure to check current best practices. At the time of writing, it is 67 characters. You can write a longer title tag, providing you keep your target keywords towards the start.

Remember that your title tag will often be shown as the first line of text for your listing in search engine results. It will also be the hyperlink to your website (or at least one page of it).

Meta description tags

Meta description tags are the two lines of text that appear below the title and URL on the search results page. Meta descriptions do not affect rankings, but they do affect click-through rates. Write your meta descriptions as you would any marketing copy — with a view to enticing the user to click through to *your* site rather than anyone else's.

Remember to include your key search terms in your meta description as this affects whether Google displays it in the results. Google also highlights in bold any of the keywords searched for. This can influence whether a user clicks on your listing.

Meta descriptions should be no more than 160 characters. You can write longer tags, but Google will crop them. This is fine, provided your key message and key search terms appear in the first 150-160 characters.

H1 tags

H1 tags are part of the HTML (HyperText Mark-up Language) code that is used to create the vast majority of websites. H1 tags are applied to the top-level headings for any content on a website page. We recommend that you only use one H1 tag per page, and that it includes your key search term(s).

It is sometimes difficult to write a heading that includes your key search terms without sounding clumsy. If you have to choose between ramming in a keyword and readability, always prefer readability.

Images

If you use an image on a web page, give it a meaningful, descriptive file name. Also, use an 'alt' tag which stands for 'alternative text' (this is another part of HTML code). The alt tag text is displayed before an image loads or when the user hovers over an image. You can use your key search term(s) in both the file name and the alt tag where it makes sense to do so. However, try not to overdo this as it could be seen as 'keyword stuffing' which Google penalises with *lower* rankings.

Content really is king

Make sure you have good quality content on your website and that you keep adding fresh content that is of interest to your target audience.

Have a good internal link structure that helps your visitors find what they want.

Keep the content on your website relevant to the key search terms you used to attract visitors to your site. Always include your key search term(s) on all, or most, of the pages. Sounds obvious, doesn't it? However, you would be surprised how many times we have had clients ask why they don't rank highly for a given search term when their page doesn't include that term!

You may hear people talk about keyword density. This is an area where you have to be careful. Google no longer uses keyword density as a *positive* ranking factor but as a *negative* one. You may find your site penalised for 'keyword stuffing' if you overuse a keyword or phrase on your page.

Make sure that your content is unique and that you do not simply use generic copy on your page. This is far easier said than done if you sell branded products alongside other resellers of the same product. If you want your branded product pages to achieve high rankings, make sure that your content and your image filenames are unique. If your supplier restricts your ability to change the product description, then *add* to the description using product reviews and other unique content.

Keep your website content fresh and up to date, as Google uses this as a ranking factor. There is no fixed rule regarding how often you should update your site's content. It will vary depending on the nature of your site. For example, you would expect news websites to update their content frequently. In contrast, if you are an engineering firm whose products don't often change then posting new content several times a day may be neither relevant nor necessary. Generally speaking, for smaller, less competitive markets, we would advise you to update your main content and add new material at least once a month.

Internal links

Internal links are how visitors navigate their way from page to page around your website. Having a focused internal link-building strategy can improve your rankings for your target search terms. Your internal links should help visitors find the content they want as easily as possible, but can also give prominence to the main pages that you want Google to rank highly. Make sure you don't dilute the strength of a page (in ranking terms) by linking to several *different* pages about the *same* subject. Do not put too many links on any given page because this comes across as artificial. While there are no strict guidelines on this, let's just say that one hundred links on a page would be too much!

Architecture

Build it right

Your site needs to be coded and designed in a way that makes it easy for search engines and visitors to navigate the content easily.

Some years ago, many sites were built using 'Flash' technology. This looked good but made it hard for search engines to index content. Flash is rather 'old news' these days and is no longer supported by Safari, Chrome and other browsers.

Use static links for the URL structure of your site as search engines find it easy to index them. Dynamic links are used when the website is built using a content management system driven by a database.

Dynamic links have two disadvantages: they are hard for people to read and can cause search engines to get stuck in a loop. Search engines get round this problem by simply not indexing any pages that cause problems — so your most important pages could be left out of searches altogether!

This is an example of a static URL:

https://www.microsoft.com

This is an example of a dynamic URL:

https://www.example.com/dynamic-page.php?page=1

I am not saying you should have an entirely static site built without a content management system! Good content management systems allow the URLs to be written in a way that is search engine friendly. Always look for this feature when you build a new website.

In today's world, with mobile devices everywhere, you must make sure that your website is 'mobile responsive' — in other words, it works well on phones and other mobile devices and adapts well to different screen sizes. In April 2015, Google declared that they would give higher rankings to websites that were optimised for mobile devices.

Figure 15: Mobile responsive example

If your site isn't already mobile responsive, you need to make sure it is as a matter of urgency.

Speed

One of the factors Google takes into account to determine rankings is a website's speed: how long it takes for your pages to load. This is important, since users tend to be impatient and will click away from sites that load slowly. You can check your website's speed with Google's tester:

https://developers.google.com/speed/pagespeed/insights/

Alternatively, you can use a speed optimisation tool like GTMetrix:

https://gtmetrix.com/

When you create your website, tell the designers or developers that they must optimise the site for speed. Aim to achieve a score of more than 85 for desktop and more than 70 for mobile.

Here are some things that you need to do to build the site for speed:

1. Choose a content management system that takes speed into account.

2. Make sure your website design is optimised for speed.

3. Keep all CSS and JavaScript in separate files and have them called in the code rather than written inline.

4. Minimise your JavaScript.

5. Minimise your CSS.

6. Set browser caching.

7. Optimise your images.

HTTPS

In 2015 Google started to rate site security as a ranking factor. It started to place even greater emphasis on this in 2016, which is why we now recommend that sites should be run under HTTPS. (HTTP stands for 'Hypertext Transfer Protocol' and HTTPS adds 'Secure' on the end). As the name implies, the HTTPS protocol provides greater security when transferring data over the web — for example, when displaying your website to the world or trading online.

To run a site under HTTPS you will need an SSL certificate. These have been in use for some time on e-commerce sites as a way to protect customer data and handle transactions securely. However, these days even non-commercial websites use SSL certificates as a way to reassure visitors that they will not compromise their own security. This is why Google favours secure sites over unsecured ones.

Robots.txt

Google works by looking at your site, working out the structure of the pages and adding these to its database. This is all done automatically using a smart bit of software called a robot (it's not really a robot but tech people sometimes need to inject a bit of glamour into their lives).

This process is called 'crawling' or 'spidering', in the sense that this little software 'robot' follows all the links on your site (or at least the ones you choose) to build an index of your pages and content.

You 'invite' Google (and other search engines) to come and 'crawl' over your site by including a robots.txt file.

This tells search engines which pages you do, or do not, want them to index. This means you can keep some pages hidden, such as pages used for internal administrative purposes. You should always include a robots.txt file on your website.

XML sitemaps

XML stands for 'Extensible Markup Language'. If you create an XML map of your website and submit it to Google, this helps them to index your site and also notifies them whenever the content changes. Google *can* index your site without an XML sitemap, but a sitemap is helpful.

301 redirects

Whenever you change a page URL (for example, from *www.yoursite.co.uk/p-169-t-shirts.apsx* to *www.yoursite.co.uk/shirts*) you need to let Google know that your page has moved or changed its name. There are a few ways to achieve this, but I recommend you use what's known as a 301 Redirect. This is the website equivalent of a signpost, telling search engines that the original page has moved permanently and can be found at a new location (URL). It also redirects all links to the old page to the new one (for example, a link from someone else's site to yours).

Ideally you want to avoid URL changes, but sometimes this is not possible for strategic or technical reasons. You need to be rigorous and make sure you have 301 Redirects in place from all the old pages — that you no longer want people to see or refer to — to the new pages.

Many companies make the mistake of listing their site both with and without the 'www' prefix. This effectively duplicates your site and dilutes your SEO. Be sure to select one option and redirect the other to the one you have selected.

Google position zero

Most businesses, naturally, want to get onto the first page of SERPs (search engine result pages), with the very first position being the ultimate target.

However, not many businesses know that Google has a position zero — in other words, a ranking *above* all the 'organic' search results (ones that are not paid for or sponsored). When someone asks Google a question, it tries to provide an answer in the form of a 'featured snippet'. This snippet appears *above* the organic search results.

To get this coveted 'position zero', you have to rethink how you write some of the copy (text) on your website. Reimagine your copy as answering the question that your customers are likely to be asking Google — especially if they aren't too sure what they want.

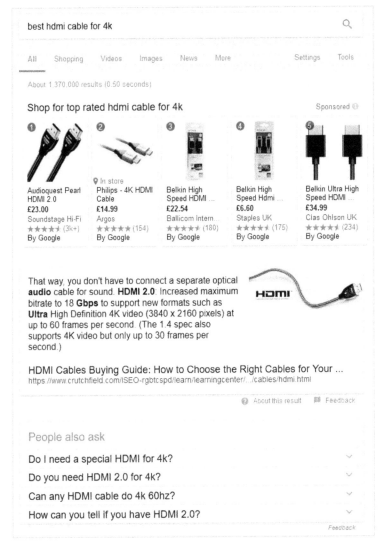

Figure 16: Example of position zero

Here's an example of a featured snippet. As you can see, all the organic results are pushed way down the page. There's the shop for HDMI cables, then the featured snippet, a list of similar questions (with other snippets), and then, below everything else, the organic search results.

In 2016, Hubspot[2] carried out a study showing that websites in position zero achieved a 114% gain in CTR (click-through rate).

How do you get to be the featured snippet?

First of all, you have to be on the first page of results. It doesn't matter what *position*, just so long as you're on that first page. In the screenshot above, the website featured in the snippet was actually third in the organic results.

Secondly, you have to have content that answers the question your target audience are most likely to ask Google. This is what Google searches for: the website most likely to provide a helpful answer. It then displays that section of copy as a featured snippet, with a link to the source – hopefully being your website.

If you've been ranking in the top ten organic results on Google, but you're struggling to break into the top spot, or even the top two, consider aiming for position zero. This may prove to be a shortcut that puts you well above your competition.

---

2 Hubspot. (2016, Febuary 09). *Hubspot*. Retrieved from Hubspot:
   https://blog.hubspot.com/marketing/how-to-featured-snippet-box

Schema markup

In 2011, the major search engines — Google, Bing and Yahoo — agreed a single schema which would improve SERPs by making such results more meaningful and informative. This is known as schema markup, structured data or microdata.

Web developers have always tried to make sure site content is formatted correctly. They do this using code that clearly conveys the *structure* of a page, for example tags like H1 and H2 specify different levels of headings. The problem with these heading tags is that they are purely *structural* and don't say what the data *means*. With the correctly applied schema markup, the data gains meaning (for example, Google will understand that a heading is actually the name of a company or product, or a movie title or whatever). Using schema markup means you're supplying more meaningful information to the search engines, which may improve your website's rankings and will definitely improve your click through rates.

Despite these clear benefits, very few businesses are implementing scheme markup so far. In 2014, Searchmetrics[3] found that only 0.3% of websites were including schema markup. More recent surveys show that this has improved to 2.7%.[4]

---

3 Searchmetrics. (2014). *Searchmetrics*. Retrieved from Searchmetrics:

https://www.searchmetrics.com/knowledge-base/schema/

4 BuiltWith. (2018, January). *Microdata Usage Statistics*. Retrieved from Builtwith:

https://trends.builtwith.com/docinfo/Microdata

Let's see how different degrees of schema markup can entice a user to click on *your* link rather than that of your competitors. Consider a simple Google search for 'chocolate brownie recipe'.

Poor

Chocolate brownie | National Trust
https://www.nationaltrust.org.uk/watersmeet/recipes/chocolate-brownie ▾
Chocolate brownie. A squidgy indulgence is what the National Trust recipe calls this treat. Follow the same recipe at home that we use in our tea garden at Watersmeet House and enjoy with your favourite cup of tea or coffee. Cakes and bakes ...

In this case, the National Trust has used no schema markup, instead relying on the content of the page to get people to click through. The uninspiring headline simply comes from the page title, with the description being pulled by Google from the copy on the page. Fortunately, it *is* relevant to the search, but it could well have been irrelevant.

Good

Best Ever Classic Chocolate Brownie Recipe - olive magazine

www.olivemagazine.com › Home › Recipes › Baking and desserts ▾
45 mins
16 Jun 2017 - Method. Heat the oven to 180C/fan 160C/gas 4. Line a 22cm square brownie tin with baking parchment. Whisk the eggs and sugar together until the mixture is light and fluffy. Fold the chocolate mixture into the egg mixture and sift on the flour, baking powder and cocoa. Fold this in to give a fudgy batter.

In this case, Olive Magazine is providing good information. There's a good use of the ingredients schema markup which you can see in the results, along with the time it should take to make the brownies. The photo makes it even more tempting to click through to the site!

Better

Best ever chocolate brownies recipe | BBC Good Food

https://www.bbcgoodfood.com/recipes/1223/bestever-brownies ▾
★★★★★ Rating 4.8 - 923 votes - 1 hr - Calories 144
Make classic chocolate brownies with this easy recipe, perfect for everyday baking and
occasions. Find more cake recipes at BBC Good Food.

BBC Good Food have done well here. They've got a tempting title and a good description. Like Olive Magazine, they also feature a tempting picture and the time it should take to create the brownies. They've also remembered to include the number of calories in their markup, and they also have reviews. All these elements make it very tempting to click on the link.

However, these three examples are taken from desktop and laptop computer screens. These results could appear very different when viewed on a mobile phone or similar device.

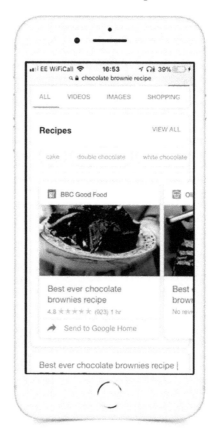

Figure 17: Rich card example

What you are seeing here is a 'rich card'. Google gives prominence to the recipe that ticks all the right boxes. The top 10 appear as scrollable cards. Some of the cards allow the searcher to send the information to their Google Home device. Now they can listen to the recipe, and also the step-by-step instructions.

All well and good, you may say, but how do chocolate brownie recipes relate to your business?

If you sell products, you should use schema markup on your website and consider including:

- An image of the product.
- A good title/headline.
- Reviews and 'star' ratings.
- A clear, helpful description.
- The price.
- The brand or manufacturer.
- Stock availability.

There's appropriate schema markup for nearly all the information a potential visitor to your site may be looking for via a search engine: blogs, news articles, events, software applications, books, job postings, courses, local businesses, restaurants, TV episodes, movies and, of course, recipes.

If you are a service business, or the purpose of your website is to generate leads rather than to sell online, then there are two key areas to mark up: site navigation and organisational data.

Site navigation markup helps search engines to understand your website structure. In turn, this means the search engines can provide clearer, more helpful results to the end user.

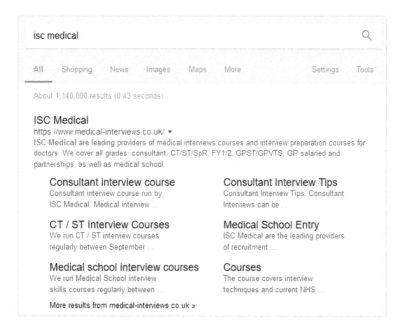

Organisation markup clarifies important information about your company's details. Your logo, company name and address should be correctly marked up using schema. This builds up your brand identity which appears in the Knowledge Graph in Google alongside the information in your Google 'My Business' listing.

If you do not use Organisation Markup, Google will try to fill the Knowledge Graph fields using publicly available information and your website content. For example, let's suppose you have several phone numbers on your home page, for customer services, technical support and sales. Let's also suppose you have some products with numerical sales codes or model numbers. How can Google be sure which is a phone number and which is a model number? If you use the correct schema markup, Google can pull the correct information into the Knowledge Graph.

Other organisational markup elements you should consider using include:

- Opening hours.

- Links to social media profiles.

- Founder.

- Founding date.

- Reviews.

- Number of employees.

- CEO/MD.

- Local business type.

- Main photo.

If you add all this information, someone using Google (or other main search engines) will see a far clearer picture of your business, with tempting imagery.

The good news is this Schema Markup is fairly easy to implement and your web developers should be able to do this for you.

You can check whether your site is correctly marked up by running your site URL through Google's Structured Data Testing Tool (*https://search.google.com/structured-data/testing-tool*).

Off-page optimisation

So far, we've been looking at search engine optimisation in terms of the elements that appear on your website's pages. The next stage is to consider elements that do *not* appear on your website but affect your rankings nonetheless. This is known as 'off-page' optimisation.

Off-page factors can be broken down into three main areas:

- External links.

- Citations and reviews.

- Social signals.

External links

Your Google ranking is affected by incoming links to your website. Google is essentially thinking, "If many trustworthy sites point to this site, then this site is also probably trustworthy". However, Google notes both the *quantity* and *quality* of these incoming links. Having lots of poor quality links will do little for your site's ranking, and may even harm it. What you really want are a significant number of good quality links. Your inbound link profile should be:

- High quality.

- Diverse.

- Relevant.

Google gives higher credit to links from sites seen as trusted or authoritative. Typical examples would be government sites or those run by educational and news organisations. In the UK, these would include .gov.uk, .ac.uk and .org.uk sites, as well as the BBC, Wikipedia, mainstream newspapers like The Telegraph and The Guardian (that are not currently behind a paywall) and so on.

Trusted sites are ones that are high quality, popular and have incoming links from authoritative sites.

If your own site isn't regarded as authoritative, it can still be classed as 'trusted'.

Your trust ranking is also affected by how long your website domain has been registered. Links from an established domain with a clean history are of greater value than links from a brand-new domain with no history.

It is very important that you never try to *buy* links. Some agencies offer to create large numbers of links to your site for a fee. This is *never* a good idea. You will just end up with all sorts of junk websites pointing to yours. What's more, Google devalues artificial and contrived incoming links. If you buy links, Google will probably find out and penalise your website, making sure it appears a long way down the search results.

Rather than buying links, attract *genuine* good quality links to your site by doing two things:

- Create good quality content that other sites will be happy to link to.

- Ask other relevant sites to link to yours.

Don't just build links to your homepage. Try and build incoming links to your internal pages.

'Anchor text' is the text featured in the hyperlink to your website. Google penalises links that are obviously contrived and based on selected keywords. If you build a natural incoming link profile (by writing killer content that people *want* to link to) then the anchor text will look natural too. When you ask sites to link to your website, ask *some* of them to use keywords but ask others to simply use your domain name, company or brand name.

Citations

Citations for SEO (where other websites point to yours as evidence) work like academic citations. An external website may mention your website, business, address, telephone number or other content without necessarily linking to you, but nonetheless clearly identifying you. These citations are good for SEO.

Social signals

'Social signals' are likes and shares on social media pages that link to your website. It is unclear whether social signals affect your search engine rankings. Nonetheless, likes and shares encourage people to visit your pages and then link to them. For this reason, it's worth building up your social media presence to strengthen your brand — which in turn will have a long-term impact on your search engine position.

Of course, good social content and comments on *trending* topics will be quickly indexed by Google.

Local SEO

If you are trying to target a local audience, there are specific things you need to do. In order to rank locally, you need to:

- Show your business name, address and phone number correctly, and make sure that you use the exact same details when you list your address on other websites.

- Obtain local reviews.

- Setup a 'Google My Business' page.

Your business name, address and phone number should appear on every page of your website and should be marked up so that search engines know how to pick up these details.

Local reviews have a direct impact on local rankings. You need to ask your customers to rate you on Google or other appropriate review sites. For example, if you run a hotel you should encourage guests to write TripAdvisor reviews (assuming they are likely to say positive things about you!).

It is also a good idea to optimise your site pages to include your city, county or area. Then look to acquire local links and citations for your website. For local SEO, the citations are normally just your business name, address and telephone number. If these appear on a number of decent sites, this can help your local ranking.

'Local' links are ones from websites in your geographical area that feature issues, events and news about your business or sector. As with all incoming links, good quality authoritative links are the ones you want. Try to acquire links sites such as the local Chamber of Commerce, industry partners and high ranking local directories.[5] [6] [7]

---

5 Moz. (2017). *The Moz Blog.* Retrieved from Moz: *https://moz.com/blog*

6 Planet Ocean. (2017). *The Unfair Advantage Book Winning the Search Engine Wars.* Retrieved from Search Engine News: *https://www.searchenginenews.com/se-news/searchenginebook/*

7 Search Engine Land. (2017). *Search Engine Land.* Retrieved from Search Engine Land: *https://searchengineland.com/*

The bottom line

- Google is still by far the most widely used search engine. It has such a substantial lead that you simply cannot ignore it and hope for good results.

- Identify the 'key' search terms most relevant to your online success.

- Build a mobile-responsive site.

- Make sure your website is built for SEO and for speed.

- Make sure your website is secure.

- Optimise your site for onsite factors:

  - Title tag.

  - Meta description tag.

  - H1 tags.

  - Images.

  - Content.

  - Domain name.

  - Architecture.

  - Robots.txt.

  - XML sitemaps.

  - 301 redirects.

  - Schema mark up.

- Provide good quality content.

- Acquire good quality links.

- Local SEO: show your business name, address and telephone number on your site and make sure this information is used accurately on other sites.

- Get customers to review your business.

- NEVER buy links.

- NEVER use spam practices.

CHAPTER 6: CONTENT IS KING

What is content marketing?

"Content marketing is the marketing and business process for creating and distributing relevant and valuable content to attract, acquire and engage a clearly defined and understood target audience with the objective of driving profitable customer action."[8]

Most people go online to find information. Providing good content is a sure way both to improve your search engine rankings and to keep your visitors engaged and coming back for more.

Focus on one content type that you build and deliver to a timetable before moving onto another content type. It takes on average 18 months to get a return on content marketing. Avoid a random approach to your content marketing. You need to be focused:

- Define your core target audience.
- Define what will be delivered.
- Define the outcome for the audience.

A good way to start is to create a blog. Many B2B companies query this, but in our experience providing new information to your target audience helps to strengthen your brand and increase sales in the long term.

---

8 Pullizi, J. (2014). *Epic Content Marketing.* McGraw Hill.

For example, consider IT Governance — a leader in IT governance, risk management and compliance. When I first started working with IT Governance, I recommended that they set up a way to capture email addresses on their new website. They did this by offering a monthly newsletter called 'Sentinel'. Today, they send out 'Sentinel' as a daily alert about cyber security issues and replicate this information on their blog. The number of subscribers has grown dramatically over the last ten years and is currently about 80,000. Each month they get about 35,000 page views and 15,000 new visitors.

Figure 18: IT Governance blog
https://www.itgovernance.co.uk/blog

Email newsletter

Email newsletters are designed to keep your customers informed about topics they are interested in. You should aim to send a newsletter out weekly or monthly. The email should be either text-based or HTML-based, with a corresponding web-based version available in case your recipient cannot read the email in their particular email client. Sending out a newsletter roundup of your blog content also works well. You can also use your newsletter to notify customers of new products or services that you are introducing.

Be sure to include a subscribe form on your website so that new visitors can sign up for your newsletter.

Whitepapers

Whitepapers cover a particular topic in depth and help you to position yourself as a thought leader. They are typically 8-10 pages long. They are particularly useful for B2B companies and work well as lead generation 'bait' (meaning that a viewer has to provide their contact details before they can download the whitepaper free of charge). Of course, you can also send your whitepaper to your existing audience or subscribers.

Ebooks

An ebook is generally longer and more comprehensive than a whitepaper. These also work well as a way to position yourself as a thought leader and for lead generation.

Case studies

A case study is a document, video or podcast that tells the story of what you achieved for a particular client. You should include the nature of the initial challenge, how you tackled it and the positive results you produced. As a document, a typical case study would be one or two pages long.

Webinar

A webinar is an online presentation. You present your content slide by slide, as you would in a regular presentation, but people watch you online or listen via telephone. You can also have pre-recorded webinars as online videos that people can watch 'on demand'.

Webinars are a good way to follow up other content such as whitepapers or ebooks.

For webinars to be successful you need to market them aggressively through your website, blog, email newsletter and social media channels.

Video

Video can be a powerful way to convey your message. However, simply having someone talk to a camera is not going to work brilliantly. You need to think about using the medium more effectively to get your point across in a powerful way.

Video is an exceptionally good way to show and demonstrate products. For example, the online clothing sector excel at using video to show off the latest fashions. It is so much easier for a customer to decide to buy a new item when they see it modelled on a catwalk! For B2B, product videos can be a highly effective way to demonstrate features and benefits. Here is a straightforward but powerful video by Ultra Dry: *https://www.youtube.com/watch?v=IPM8OR6W6WE.*

The Official Ultra-Ever Dry Video - Superhydrophobic coating - Repels almost any liquid!

UltraTech International, Inc.

12,130,108 views

Figure 19: Ultra-Ever Dry video

Great video content can also contribute to your SEO. Search engines regard video as quality content that wins a higher page ranking. However, you need to optimise your video for search engines by adding a title, description, tags and a transcript. In addition, use video schema markup and submit a video XML sitemap to search engines.

You can find Google's schema markup for videos here:

https://developers.google.com/webmasters/videosearch/sch ema

Podcasts

Podcasts are audio files that your listeners can download and listen to whenever they wish. They typically last 5-30 minutes and they work best as a series that your listeners can download daily, weekly or monthly. There has been some discussion about whether, in this age of video, podcasts will have much traction. However, this depends on your target market. I have seen some B2B businesses run podcasts as a very effective way to grow their audience.

Infographics

An infographic uses a combination of text and graphics to present factual information in a visually striking way. For example, you could create one that clarifies a technical issue or summarises the key points about something in the news that is relevant to your business. Take care to produce your infographic in a way that is easy to share online.

You can produce your infographics in-house, using tools such as Piktochart, or outsource this work to an agency. If you do create your own, you may like to know that sites such as iStock now provide images you can use for your Infographics.

Figure 20: The history of content marketing infographic[9]

---

9 *https://contentmarketinginstitute.com/2012/02/history-content-marketing-infographic/*

Online surveys

Online surveys can be an excellent way to gather material that you can later present as a report. There are several online survey tools you can use, such as Survey Monkey, and some are even free. Digital marketing and e-commerce research specialists, Econsutlancy[10], produce top quality survey reports such as 'Digital Intelligence Briefing: 2017 Digital Trends in IT', or, 'State of B2B Marketing Automation'.

Online press releases

Online press releases, as the name suggests, are simply press releases that you publish online. They help you to build your brand and drive traffic to your site. Links from press releases are marked as 'no-follow' links so Google does not take them into account.

Online press releases are a good way to get coverage in relevant media and to get mentioned on sites your target audiences are likely to visit.

Create a monthly or quarterly schedule for your online press releases and always make sure they are newsworthy.

When writing your press release, always start by identifying its purpose. Your press release should:

- Identify your story, such as:

    - A new product or service.

    - A strategic partnership.

---

10 Econsultancy. (2018, January). *Econsultancy*. Retrieved from Econsultancy: *https://econsultancy.com/*

- An award.

- A new book you've published.

- Release of new software.

- Adoption of innovative industry techniques.

- Major new contracts.

- Charitable sponsorship.

- Provide information to answer the questions:

  - Who?

  - What?

  - When?

  - Where?

  - Why?

  - How?

Include data, images, videos and quotes as this improves the chances of the release being shared. Make sure you include links to your site to generate traffic (not for SEO purposes). Include contact details so that journalists can get in touch.

Submit your press release to an online service such as PR Web (*http://uk.prweb.com/*) or PR Fire (*http://www.prfire.com/*). Make sure you publish your release via your blog and social media.

The bottom line

- Develop a content marketing plan.

- Define your core target audience.

- Define what will be delivered.

- Define the outcome for the audience.
- Stick to your plan.

CHAPTER 7: SOCIAL MEDIA MARKETING

Valuable opportunities

Social media marketing involves engaging your target market via social media to increase brand awareness and, ultimately, to get people to buy your products or services. If you don't currently use social media for marketing purposes, you can be sure that someone will suggest it: your agency, your marketing executive or even your son or daughter!

You may be rather sceptical at first, but it's important to understand just how effective this can be. Social media has transformed the way people live and communicate. It has changed how relationships work, how we consume media and how we get our daily news. There's no doubt that most brands can benefit from having an online social presence. It's important that you don't miss out on the many opportunities provided by social media.

The first thing is to define where social media fits into your overall marketing strategy. Then define the resources you need to set up, run and manage your social media campaigns.

Set up a plan for the year and then define your content. Depending on how frequently you post to social media, it may be practical to define the content quarterly in advance.

Some businesses dive into social media without a content strategy, which is not a good move. First, determine your content strategy and let this drive your social media marketing strategy.

In defining your strategy, you need to evaluate which social media sites would work best for your business. They tend to have particular 'niche' marketing appeal, so it's good to identify the ones that would work best for your brand. You may also want to consider their relative market share:

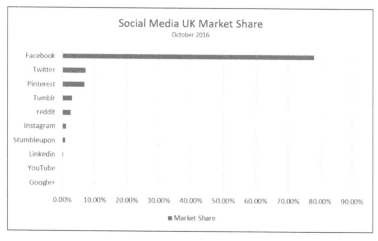

Figure 21: Source Statista

From the graph above you might conclude that you should work exclusively with Facebook. However, don't be too quick to dismiss the less popular sites. Their lower percentage market share masks the difference in demographics and interests of the people that use them. For example, take Reddit. If you are in the IT industry, it would be a very good idea to make sure your content is picked up on Reddit. Getting on to the front page of Reddit is likely to guarantee a significant increase in traffic to your website.

For B2C businesses, it is a bit of a 'no-brainer' to make sure you have an active Facebook presence. Facebook has changed the way the home feed works so brands get much less exposure than they did before. This means you have to advertise on Facebook to get your content seen. I suggest you make this an important part of your social media strategy.

If your products are suited to great photography, then having a suitable strategy for Instagram, or perhaps Pinterest, would be useful.

I strongly advise any B2B company to have a strategy for LinkedIn. I see many businesses in diverse B2B sectors using it successfully to generate leads.

Although Twitter is suffering from stagnating growth, I have nonetheless seen successful B2C and B2B strategies that embrace it. Many high-profile brands use Twitter for customer service – for example Asda, Carphone Warehouse and Virgin Trains.

While Facebook is seen primarily as a B2C channel, a quarter of buyers said they would use Facebook to influence their buying decision. This is higher than the number who would use Twitter or LinkedIn.[11]

Examples of social media marketing

Here are some examples I have seen:

Innocent Smoothies/Facebook

One UK brand that uses social media very effectively is Innocent Smoothies. They are a brand found in every supermarket, with a fairly simple product. Why are they such a good example of how to use social media marketing? It all comes down to the marketing message and the voice. Much

---

11 Hotwire. (2016). *Changing Face of Influencers.*

of their communications are light-hearted and humorous. They engage with their followers on a regular basis and are always active. Also, they are not afraid to go 'off-brand' and discuss things entirely irrelevant to their product, such as commenting on TV shows via Twitter. This may not be directly marketing smoothies, but it definitely helps with their branding.

One of their big social media campaigns is "The Big Knit". You can see a sample post below.

innocent
Yesterday at 08:00 ·

The innocent Big Knit is back. Little woolly hats. On our smoothies. In shops everywhere. NOW. Each one raises money for Age UK so they can be there for older people.

Figure 22: innocent Facebook woolly hat campaign

While this isn't the best example of an Innocent Smoothie social media post, I have chosen it because it encapsulates a lot of good ideas:

- Use of subtle humour, even though it's a serious cause.

- Top photography that is on-brand, interesting and actually features the product.

- Creates a sense of community among followers, creating 'brand evangelists'.

- Opportunity for fans to share their own hats.

- Giving to a good cause, which is central to the Innocent brand.

- Tagging of another brand (Age UK) to create cross-brand engagement.

- A special offer unique to this campaign.

Of course, Facebook lends itself to B2C audiences. But B2B brands can also benefit from the extensive targeting available through Facebook advertisements.

Coca-Cola/Facebook

Figure 23 shows another example involving Facebook.

Figure 23: Coca-Cola Facebook recycling campaign

As one of the biggest brands on the planet, it's no surprise that Coca-Cola puts a lot of effort into its social presence. All businesses, large or small, can learn something from the huge corporations that generate good content for social media. This can be as simple as uploading photos made for the platform, uploading video clips from within the business, or posting links to other forms of content.

Facebook loves video content, and Coca-Cola puts considerable effort into making high quality, short, watchable video clips. The example shown here amassed 81,000 views in a day, so you can see the appeal in terms of engagement. This video content could also be reused across different channels and for different marketing campaigns.

One thing that makes business owners worry about using social media is the possibility of getting negative reviews. It's true that social media may open your brand to abuse. However, there are good ways to handle these responses, as Coca-Cola demonstrates here in the comments under the same video:

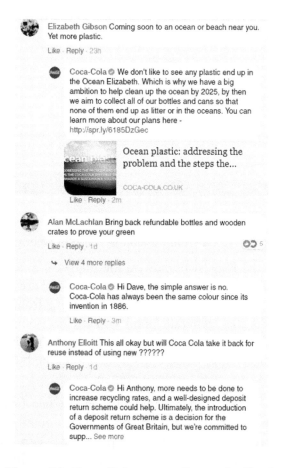

Figure 24: Coca-Cola responding to feedback

You can see the way Coca-Cola actively engages with the concerns raised by the public — both fans and non-fans alike.

While this is a huge organisation that is likely to have a social media team, smaller organisations can still learn many valuable lessons from them.

Domino's/Facebook Messenger

But Facebook is more than just one social platform. It owns Facebook's own Messenger, WhatsApp, Instagram, and more. So, what does the future hold for the wider Facebook platform?

Consider a company such as Domino's, who now use the Messenger app to take orders.

Figure 25: Domino's Pizza messenger campaign

Hungry customers don't need to ring or even go online to order their pizza. They can simply talk to an artificial intelligence 'bot' that will complete the order for them.

While this may be a strange concept to some, it is likely to become much more common in the future. Many brands use Facebook for customer queries, and will complete sales through the chat functionality of Facebook Messenger. But if you can have automated replies from a bot that handles frequently-asked questions, or can complete orders, this is far more effective.

Social media networks are evolving all the time, and social media marketing will evolve alongside them. Messenger apps have become widely used, and texting has already become an outdated concept for many youngsters.

Virgin Atlantic/Twitter

Figure 26: Virgin Atlantic Twitter campaign

It's easy to make holidays look good. However, specific aspects of the tweet shown here help Virgin Atlantic's social media strategy pay off.

The product is an easy sell, but they are generating content (related to their product) that people want to watch.

In this case, it's a video showing how Virgin Atlantic is aiming to put Tobago on the map as an authentic Caribbean experience: *"Working with Tobago's Ministry of Tourism, we travelled to the island to see it for ourselves. There, we found a living, thriving culture — one rich with some of nature's most stunning vistas and the Caribbean's most colourful personalities. We had a combined team of 60 crew and locals to help us out, spending over 60 hours capturing beautiful content - and really got to the heart of what the island can offer for a Caribbean getaway."*

This video is clearly enough to capture the attention of the public. As part of a wider campaign, it taps into the kind of content people want to see. The notion of a 'hidden gem' always intrigues travellers, and people like to look at images or videos online when they are planning their holidays. Videos capture the attention and keep people engaged for longer. This particular example is also a cross promotion with Google Street View. Of course, this campaign also benefits the island of Tobago, so it has a 'feel-good' factor.

It's not hard to see why Virgin put so much effort into their social media content. 82% of Twitter users watch video content on Twitter (*https://www.bloomberg.com/news/articles/2016-04-28/snapchat-user-content-fuels-jump-to-10-billion-daily-video-views*), and it's becoming a growing part of the platform. As a campaign, this message encourages people to book holidays in Tobago, plus it gives the brand a good image of finding 'hidden gem' destinations that other holiday companies might not know about. The brand also benefits from being seen to help the Tobago tourism industry, thereby improving the lives of the people that live there.

BT/Twitter

BT successfully use Twitter as a key customer service tool, using it to both answer questions and address customer complaints.

Customers love being able to get instant replies, without the need to wait for an email to arrive or someone to answer a phone call.

The fact that Twitter posts are public offers both benefits and drawbacks. As a brand, you are publicly seen to be dealing with customer queries on a regular basis, which instils confidence in what you have to offer. On the other hand, people may occasionally see dissatisfied customers saying bad things about you. However, you do get the chance to address complaints in a helpful, constructive way that may salvage the situation and create a favourable impression. This is better than negative reviews appearing in places where you don't have any means of replying.

In 2014, customer service via social media deflected 600,000 contacts a year from phones, which led to £2 million in annual savings.

https://econsultancy.com/blog/68167-30-brands-with-excellent-social-media-strategies

Starbucks/Instagram

As a brand, Starbucks strongly identifies with the 'Instagram' generation. It therefore comes as no surprise that their Instagram account is pretty spot on for B2C audiences.

Figure 27: Starbucks Instagram page

Turning something as simple as a cup of coffee and a cake into a picture worthy of note is something Starbucks excel at, which is one reason why they have a loyal following across the world.

Starbucks has an enthusiastic fanbase of social media users who share their latest treats or drinks on Instagram and elsewhere, and the company's own Instagram account is an excellent way to engage with them.

Couple this with marketing campaigns featuring 'special edition' coffees, available for a limited time only, that drives its fans to its numerous outlets, and you can see why Starbucks social media marketing is so effective.

There's also the persistent rumour that Starbuck's baristas misspell customer names on purpose to win mentions on social media! Whether it's true or not, it's free advertising!

Salesforce/Instagram

B2B companies can also make good use of Instagram. For example, Salesforce shares all kinds of content on Instagram and has established a strong following.

While they are clearly a big enough brand to warrant such a following, you can see just how much the content differs from more B2C-orientated content. It has a much warmer, personal tone. Who doesn't love behind-the-scenes photos of big companies and cute photos of dogs?

Figure 28: Salesforce Instagram page

Adobe/LinkedIn

LinkedIn is important for most brands, especially B2B. While it may not be a suitable fit for some B2C brands, it is still good to have a LinkedIn presence if you are looking to recruit, or perhaps to share company news with industry peers.

Adobe is a household name that does a fine job of marketing on LinkedIn.

Adobe post a lot of visual content that blends business news and behind-the-scenes updates with industry insights and helpful content. They also use the platform for recruitment, creating content intended to excite potential employees about what it would be like to work for the company.

Figure 29: Adobe LinkedIn pages

If your business can create and share B2B focused content on LinkedIn, it's a great way to build brand awareness and generate leads or sales. In a B2B space, your target audience is more likely to be active on LinkedIn (or at least to check in regularly) than many other platforms. Facebook is more personal in nature and is mostly used for communicating with family and friends. Twitter tends to be used by younger audiences for news and updates. LinkedIn provides a unique opportunity to reach professionals in related fields or industries that are important to your brand.

If your content is good enough to get shared by peers, industry experts and colleagues on LinkedIn, this is great news for your social media marketing. Get the content right, and people in your industry will happily share it among themselves — effectively doing your publicity for you!

When it comes to B2B advertising, LinkedIn provides a way to target precisely the companies you want to reach. They may charge more than other platforms, but this precision means the ROI can be far higher.

LinkedIn also gives you an opportunity to create relevant groups and foster industry-specific discussions.

NASA/Snapchat

Snapchat grew from a simple image sharing app to a messaging and social platform. Being able to follow celebrities, brands and anyone else on Snapchat has revolutionised its potential. For many brands, Snapchat is the perfect platform to showcase what they are up to. If your audience consists of millennials or younger audiences, then Snapchat is a great place to be. It's simple to set-up your account and create photo or video content. However, it is very different from other social platforms as it consists solely of visual content that expires after 24 hours. It's worth considering that Snapchat users watch about 10 *billion* videos a day (*http://www.adweek.com/digital/snapchatters-watch-10-billion-videos-every-day-171130/*), though it is currently in a period of stagnation while it works out how to truly monetize the platform. Nonetheless, it's still a very powerful and popular messaging app and social platform used by people all around the world.

For instance, NASA use it to stay relevant and show the world what they are up to.

Figure 30: NASA Snapchat story

7: Social media marketing

When the International Space Station was celebrating 100,000 orbits, NASA used Snapchat to document the daily life of the crew on board. They created a series of clips with annotations and jokes that really captured the imagination of viewers (*https://www.engadget.com/2016/05/17/nasa-snapchat-live-story/*).

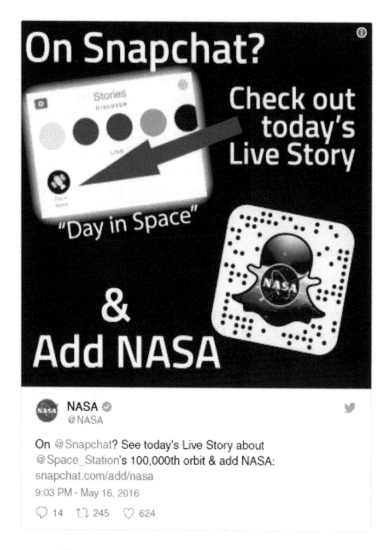

Figure 31: NASA cross-promotion on Twitter

As you can see, NASA cross-promoted this event on Twitter to broaden their fanbase. So why is it significant that they are using Snapchat?

Snapchat is most popular among younger people and is a great way to build a sense of belonging to an 'exclusive' club. NASA therefore created content stylised to appeal to a younger audience, rather than seasoned scientists. Would many scientists understand the 'Wingardium Leviosa' reference to Harry Potter in one of the snaps? Probably not — but it's sure to resonate with millennial audiences. Of course, NASA have content elsewhere that appeals to more serious audiences or older generations, but this is a good example of how a brand can use different platforms to reach different market niches.

Campaigns

Many business owners find it difficult to decide what to upload and share with the world on a regular basis. After all, there are only so many company updates or staff outings you can put on Facebook. This is where your social media marketing strategy comes into play.

Social media is more than just picking a network and posting business updates. People want to see content or updates they find useful and entertaining.

In today's online world, the right campaign for your brand can go 'viral' and reach thousands or even millions of viewers. Many businesses try to achieve this kind of viral awareness through 'growth hacking'. This is simply another term for digital marketing which aims to replicate explosive growth or exposure online. Going viral takes good quality content, an engaged audience and — to be frank — a fair amount of luck. But putting together a good social media marketing campaign will greatly increase your chances of 'going viral'.

Let's consider what kind of campaigns go viral.

A good example is IKEA's Place app. IKEA promote this app as their latest effort to, "perhaps change the way people buy furniture forever". Their highly innovative app engages their huge customer base, and led to a viral social media campaign with next to no work on their part.

IKEA fans are everywhere and they use social media a lot. Once they got a hold of this new Place app, they were placing virtual furniture everywhere and sharing screenshots and videos on Twitter and other social platforms. IKEA didn't need to do anything to spread the news about their new app because it was amusing in itself.

As for brands that have created a business out of social media, there are plenty of examples.

Take Joe Wicks, 'The Body Coach'. While he has a TV show and line of fitness books now, he achieved much of his early exposure via social media posts. He posts simple recipes and shows people how to make them, tapping into the widespread interest in eating healthy food that tastes great and helps you to lose weight. By providing great value, and posting photos that people like to look at, he has created a brand that people want to engage with. Other companies can learn from similar personalities that have created their own brand through consistent and authentic social media engagement.

Figure 32: Joe Wicks' Instagram page

Take a look at the Joe Wicks Instagram feed. It features a mixture of personal posts, recipes, submissions from fans and product placement — all via photos and videos. He's amassed 2 million followers who will likely join his weight loss programme, buy his books, watch his shows and engage with his content.

In similar vein, on the viral side, consider an example such as 'Salt Bae'. This was a simple video of a restaurant owner, named Nusret Gökçe, showing off his talents with a knife and seasoning meat. This became a must-watch video for the social media generation, spawning many different remixes and tributes:

http://metro.co.uk/2018/01/16/salt-bae-open-first-new-york-steakhouse-7232615/

The viral success of Nusret's videos led to him opening a New York steakhouse with his name emblazoned on the side! He is the embodiment of what viral content can do for business.

The beauty of this example is that it was so simple and effective. It's doubtful that Nusret *intended* to achieve this level of fame, but it certainly worked. With very little strategy, style or budget, his early videos became a social media sensation.

This just goes to show that if you have something unique that's interesting or amusing, people will watch. How *many* people watch will depend on your marketing and a little bit of luck. The Salt Bae video picked up 2.4 million views in just two days. At the time of writing, it's at 4 million views, while the restaurant owner himself has 10.5 million followers on Instagram — all this largely because of one video. However, don't think that you need to 'go viral' to enjoy success on social media. This is simply not true. Going viral is something many business owners get carried away with, but it takes a good amount of luck and timing.

Open graph tags

There's no doubt that many companies embrace the power of a social media, from small start-ups to the largest blue chip. They all see the power and benefits of people liking and sharing their content. Some sites even *require* you to like their Facebook page or Twitter account before you can read their content or download a whitepaper.

However, for a long time there was a significant problem. Suppose someone liked your website and wanted to tell their friends about it. They clicked the 'Share' button... and got a random image and some confusing text that wasn't quite what they wanted to share. The 'Share' function was completely automated and, in trying to figure out what the visitor wanted to share, it could make mistakes and 'scrape' the wrong content from your page. The frustrated visitor, unable to edit or over-ride the 'Share' function, simply abandoned the idea. They didn't share your content because it would have looked odd to their friends and followers.

This was the case before Open Graph tags were invented. Open graph tags give you *some* control over what happens when people try to link to your page or specific content. By adding a few meta tags, you can make sure that when visitors want to share your content on Facebook, Twitter and other social media platforms, your link appears the way you would like it to. You can control the image that gets shared, title, copy, URL and lots more. This makes your site easier to share and means that what gets shared is accurate and well displayed.

Use Open Graph tags wherever you want to encourage people to share your content. It makes life easier for them and for you.

Summary

For many businesses, social media plays a significant role in generating trade. Even if it doesn't generate direct sales, it's an important way of keeping their brand relevant in the fast-moving, competitive online world.

Maybe your brand won't get direct sales from social media. Maybe you think it's a waste of time and money. But if your business isn't visible on social media, many customers may conclude that you aren't 'legitimate' or worth their time.

Many people now go to Twitter or Facebook for enquiries, and if your brand isn't there, they could forget dealing with you altogether. If they come across an old, out-of-date social media profile, this can also leave a bad impression of your brand.

If you aren't convinced that allocating part of your marketing budget to social media is worthwhile, it's at least worth setting up profiles and have them ticking over in the background.

However, if you can really master social media marketing — as part of your overall digital marketing strategy — you're very likely to discover a new channel that can boost your revenue.

The bottom line

- Pick the social media channels relevant for your business and consider at least LinkedIn for B2B and Facebook for B2C.

- Because of its reach, don't ignore Facebook.

- Create a social media plan and stick to it.

- Test, measure and refine.

CHAPTER 8: EMAIL OR FAIL

Email and ROI

If you often feel overwhelmed by incoming emails, you may be tempted to dismiss email as an effective form of marketing. However, according to the latest email marketing report by Adestra and Econsultancy (2016)[12] **email marketing has the highest return on investment.**

List acquisition

Before you start any email campaigns you have to have a list of email addresses *and* permission from everyone on it to send them emails.

The most effective email marketing lists are ones that you have built up over time from your own customers and prospects. If you are an established B2B company, you probably already have a good 'starter' list of your customers and prospects. If you are in B2C and run a bricks and mortar store, you need to create a way to gather email addresses from customers. The simplest way is to ask customers as they are paying for goods if they also want to sign up to your email list. To prompt them to do this, as with all marketing, think about what is in it for them and offer something in exchange. One effective approach is to say, "We sometimes run special offers and product giveaways. Would you like to be notified when we do?". Most customers will happily provide their email address if you ask them in this way.

---

12 Adestra, E. a. (2016). *Email Marketing Industry Census 2016.*

The other place to acquire email addresses is of course on your website. I always recommend that you ask visitors to your website to sign up for email offers or news depending on what works for your business. Increasingly, online retailers are doing this within seconds of you visiting their homepage. Look at this example on Mango's website:

Figure 33: Mango sign up form
https://shop.mango.com/gb

Retailers do this because they understand the *lifetime value* of a customer. They know that someone who visits their site for the first time, even if they do not buy anything, may return later — especially if prompted to do so by news of a special offer or promotion. What's more, the amount they spend during the time they remain a customer will be far more than if they only visited and bought something once, never to return.

Some retailers remain sceptical about email marketing because they think no-one opens or reads marketing emails. It's true that many marketing emails are ignored. However, if you send an email that's directly relevant to whatever a customer is thinking of buying, they will almost certainly read it and visit your site. Think about it from the customers' perspective. In some cases, it's really nice and helpful to get ideas and prompts. Suppose someone is trying to decide which Christmas presents to buy for toddlers. They will certainly appreciate an email headed '20 New Toy Ideas for a Fantastic Toddler Christmas'.

B2B businesses can take a different tack, such as offering industry news, technical whitepapers or ebooks in exchange for an email address. For Vigilant Software, we used one of Justin Brooke's landing page layouts for downloading a whitepaper. Note how well this is constructed, from the wording to the layout. Once you click on 'Download Now' or 'Yes! Send me the free whitepaper', you are presented with a simple form to complete.

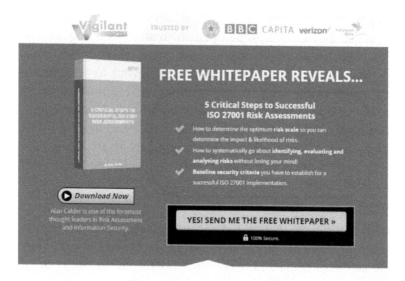

Figure 34: Vigilant Software whitepaper download landing page

The FREE whitepaper will be sent to the
email address you submit above!

Figure 35: Vigilant Software whitepaper download form

We built this download form as part of a 'funnel' for the company. The results were a 61% increase in downloads and 10x increase in sales.

You can also buy or rent lists, but your own lists will always yield greater results than lists you acquire. If you do buy or rent a list, you must only use lists that comply with the GDPR.

Email campaigns

The three most common forms of email campaigns are:

- Product or service promotions.
- Sale offers.

- Newsletters.

Email is an excellent way to notify your customers of new products or service launches in both B2B and B2C. Sale offers are used heavily in B2C and sometimes in B2B.

In B2B, newsletters are used primarily to keep customers up-to-date with events in the industry. A good example is the IT Governance daily newsletter, Sentinel, which details the latest information security issues including security breaches and changes in legislation. IT Governance started building their list by asking visitors to their website if they wanted to subscribe to what was initially a monthly newsletter. Increasing concerns about cyber security issues led to the newsletter becoming so popular that it became a daily publication.

In B2C, I have seen a trend towards more inventive email campaigns. For example, as well as straightforward sales promotions, some companies are featuring customer stories to add 'human interest'. One such company is The Fold, which specialises in clothing for professional women. It ran a campaign with the subject, "The Fold Woman – A Celebration of Career, Ambition, Life and Style". It profiled Emma Heal, Retail Director of Graze.com, and included three of Emma's favourite outfits.

Figure 36: The Fold email campaign

As I have said, email campaigns start with an email list. The next step is to plan your campaign. Plan each campaign monthly, quarterly or annually in advance and stick to your plan! This does not mean you have to be inflexible — you should always be ready to accommodate breaking news that might affect your business. For example, IT Governance plan the content of their daily newsletter well in advance, but if a big cyber attack is in the news they mention it in the next email they send out.

As with all digital marketing, start with your client in mind. By now you will have crafted one or more personas for your business. Make sure you start with your chosen persona and build your email campaigns accordingly.

Your target persona, brand positioning and corporate values will define the tone of voice that's appropriate for your email campaigns.

IT Governance know they are talking to CISOs and CIOs who need to be kept abreast of everything to do with information security governance, risk and compliance. They use a serious, informed tone because they are addressing serious issues to an audience that has the unenviable task of managing their company's cyber risk.

By contrast, Innocent Smoothies use a tone that's simple, clear and fun across all their marketing, while The Fold know their customer is a professional woman who identifies with their tagline, 'Empowering Professional Women'.

Subject lines

You need to spend nearly as much time crafting the subject line of your email to appeal to your audience as you do writing the email. There has been a lot of research on this and our own experience shows that the subject line is the biggest single factor determining whether people will open your email or not.

For B2C, enticing email subject lines work well, as do special offers. For B2B, our research shows that emails work best when the subject line does what it says on the tin — B2B audiences do not respond well to sensational subject lines.

Personalisation

You can personalise both the subject line and the body of the emails you send out. Many travel companies do this well, using your selected preferences to tailor their campaigns to your specific needs.

People have become so used to personalisation that they now more or less expect it. This means you need to go beyond simple list segmentation and work towards personalising your emails as much as you can.

In order to deliver a personalised experience, you need tools that allow you to gather information about your customer and deliver dynamic content accordingly. Marketing automation integrated with a CRM gives you the ability to do this.

Some examples of useful marketing automation are:

- Abandoned basket emails for e-commerce sites.
- Date notifications.
- Timed content programmes through the sales cycle.

Landing pages

In 2006, Bryan Eisenberg[13] coined a phrase that is still applicable today: "Follow the scent". What he means is that when a customer clicks through from your email to your website, they need to see what they saw in the email. If you send an email showing your latest product, the customer who clicks through to your site should arrive at the relevant product page or a category page featuring that product. This should hold true across all devices. If a customer opens your email on their mobile phone, they should be taken straight to the relevant page, or at least a version of that page optimised for mobile phone display.

Mobile

At the risk of labouring the point, your email campaigns should be mobile responsive. Given the extent to which people rely on their phones these days, especially for accessing emails, it is essential that your email campaigns are mobile responsive. You also need to allow for the fact that we live in a rather fast-paced, attention-deficit world! Make sure you get your key message across quickly, with a prominent call to action.

Test, measure and refine

You need to be able to assess your email marketing effectiveness using the lead indicators of open rates and click-through rates. You should be able to get this information from your email marketing platform.

---

13 Eisenberg, B. (n.d.). *Call to Action.* ebook

8: Email or fail

'Open rate' means the number of people who opened your email as a percentage of the emails you sent.

'Click-through rate' means the number of people who clicked the link in the email as a percentage of the total emails you sent.

SmartInsights maintain benchmark open rates and click-through rates by industry for small- to medium-sized businesses. The figures make for interesting reading.

Industry	Open rate (%)	Clickthrough rate (%)
Agriculture and Food Services	24.71%	2.98%
Architecture and Construction	24.78%	2.90%
Arts and Artists	27.23%	2.85%
Beauty and Personal Care	18.48%	1.96%
Business and Finance	20.97%	2.73%
Computers and Electronics	20.87%	2.16%
Construction	22.10%	1.95%
Consulting	19.54%	2.26%
Creative Services/Agency	22.41%	2.61%
Daily Deals/E-Coupons	15.22%	2.39%

8: Email or fail

Industry	Open rate (%)	Clickthrough rate (%)
E-commerce	16.75%	2.32%
Education and Training	22.00%	2.63%
Entertainment and Events	21.21%	2.33%
Gambling	18.75%	3.35%
Games	20.82%	3.33%
Government	26.33%	3.62%
Health and Fitness	21.93%	2.57%
Hobbies	28.46%	5.13%
Home and Garden	23.82%	3.47%
Insurance	21.56%	2.11%
Legal	22.49%	2.99%
Manufacturing	21.74%	2.33%
Marketing and Advertising	17.81%	1.92%
Media and Publishing	22.14%	4.70%
Medical, Dental, and Healthcare	22.43%	2.42%
Mobile	19.43%	2.10%

8: Email or fail

Industry	Open rate (%)	Clickthrough rate (%)
Music and Musicians	22.86%	2.84%
Non-Profit	24.98%	2.76%
Other	23.06%	2.81%
Pharmaceuticals	20.02%	2.51%
Photo and Video	25.36%	3.49%
Politics	22.23%	2.17%
Professional Services	20.89%	2.47%
Public Relations	20.12%	1.64%
Real Estate	20.84%	1.91%
Recruitment and Staffing	20.73%	2.18%
Religion	26.46%	3.11%
Restaurant	21.17%	1.25%
Restaurant and Venue	21.71%	1.33%
Retail	20.96%	2.50%
Social Networks and Online Communities	21.71%	3.33%

Industry	Open rate (%)	Clickthrough rate (%)
Software and Web App	20.95%	2.29%
Sports	25.41%	3.19%
Telecommunications	21.57%	2.43%
Travel and Transportation	20.69%	2.17%
Vitamin Supplements	17.26%	1.80%

Figure 37: Email engagement rates for small to medium businesses[14]

While 'open' and 'click through' rates tell you a lot, what you ultimately want to measure is conversions (how many actually bought something from you). If you are using marketing automation, you will be able to get this data from your platform. Alternatively, or in addition to your own figures, you should be able to measure your email marketing effectiveness through Google Analytics.

---

14 SmartInsights. (2017). *Email Marketing Statistics 2017.* Retrieved from SmartInsights: *http://www.smartinsights.com/email-marketing/email-communications-strategy/statistics-sources-for-email-marketing/*

Email marketing platforms

There are a number of email marketing platforms for SMEs. PC Mag reviewed the top 10. Here is their list:[15]

1. Campaign Monitor

2. Constant Contact

3. SendinBlue

4. GetResponse

5. Zoho Campaigns

6. Infusionsoft

7. Campaigner

8. MailChimp

9. Pardot

10. Hubspot

We find most clients prefer Campaign Monitor, Constant Contact or MailChimp. Our own experience is that Campaign Monitor is unbelievably easy to use and the integration with Google Analytics and social media is simple, straightforward and fast to implement.

Many of our clients have now moved onto marketing automation and now use SharpSpring for their email campaigns. See the chapter on Marketing Automation for further details.

---

15 PC Mag. (2017). *The Best Email Marketing Software of 2017*. Retrieved from PC Mag: *http://uk.pcmag.com/e-mail-products/3708/guide/the-best-email-marketing-software-of-2017*

The bottom line

- Build a good quality list.
- Develop an email marketing plan and stick to it.
- Make sure your email campaigns are mobile responsive and the calls to action work on multiple channels.
- Use a good marketing automation platform.
- Use your platform's advanced personalisation tools.
- Test, measure and refine.
- Make sure you comply with the GDPR and Privacy Regulations.

CHAPTER 9: IT'S WISE TO ADVERTISE

The rise and rise of paid advertising

Paid advertising has come a long way since Google AdWords first offered pay per click (PPC) adverts on its search engine and third-party websites.

While Bing offers another platform similar to Google AdWords for search advertising, the real game changer in recent years has been Facebook's introduction of paid online advertising. Other social media platforms like LinkedIn, Twitter, Pinterest, Tumblr and Snapchat also offer paid advertising. Instagram and YouTube advertising are covered by Facebook and Google respectively.

I will focus on Google AdWords and Facebook because of their enormous market share of UK online advertising. In 2015, Google and Facebook accounted for 64% of the global digital advertising market.[16]

Google AdWords

Google AdWords allows you to run adverts on search engines or on third-party websites. This allows you to advertise your products or services either at the precise moment someone is looking for them, or when they visit other relevant sites.

Pay per click advertising gives you the ability to:

---

16 Bloomberg Technology. (2016, April 22). Google and Facebook Lead Digital Ad
   Industry to Revenue Record.

- Attract more customers.

- Reach the right people at the right time.

- Target your ads locally or globally.

Search ads

Search ads appear on search engine results pages when a surfer uses a particular search term or keyword, such as 'recruitment services'. If you have chosen that term (more about how later on) for your ad, then your ad may appear at the top of the organic search results. I say *may* appear because it depends on three factors that Google takes into account: your quality score, your bid and the bids of your competitors. You pay Google (or Bing) each time a user clicks on your ad, hence the term 'pay per click' (PPC).

Your quality score is a score from 1-10 assessing the quality of your ad and your landing page. The higher your score, the lower your click cost is likely to be.

Your bid is the amount you tell Google that you are willing to pay per click for each keyword. This is known as Cost Per Click (CPC) bidding. There are other bidding methods such as Cost Per Impression (CPM) (normally per 1000 impressions) used in display advertising and Cost Per Acquisition (CPA).

Competition reflects the quality and bids of competing advertisers for your chosen keywords.

Keyword research

If you use a Google AdWords campaign, you obviously want to make sure that you target the right people. The first step is to research the keywords people will use when searching for your products or services. To do this, you need to open a Google AdWords account so you can use their keyword tool. However, this is only the starting point.

Match type

Once you have selected your keywords, you need to select the right match type, depending on what you are trying to achieve with your ads. There are four match types:

Broad

This is the default match type.

Syntax: plain text, e.g., women's hats

Impact: will match synonyms, misspellings, related search terms and similar terms. For example, Google will show your ad to anyone who searches for 'buy ladies hats'.

Modified broad

Syntax: qualify your term with +. Example: +women's +hats

Impact: will only show your ad to searches that contain the specified words or close variations, e.g., 'hats for women'.

Phrase

Syntax: qualify with " ". Example: "women's hats"

Impact: will only show your ad to searches containing the specified phrase or a close variation of that phrase. In recent times, many users have preferred Modified Broad Match over Phrase Match.

Exact

Syntax: qualify with [ ]. Example: [women's hats]

Impact: will only show your ad to searches that exactly match the term you have specified or close variations.

Negative match

In addition to these options, there is also the Negative Match option, meaning you can specify keywords you do *not* want to match with. For example, you might want to make sure your ad doesn't appear if someone includes 'free' in their search (because you aren't interested in people who aren't willing to pay for your product). Intelligent use of negative keywords helps you to control your costs and improve the performance of your campaigns.

Syntax: qualify with –. Example: -free

Impact: will not show ads for searches including the word 'free'

Example strategies

You choose your positive match types according to your business objectives. For example, if you sell cameras you might devise a strategy like this:

Broad match: digital camera

Landing page: useful content on selecting a digital camera, or a comparison table of the top ten digital cameras.

Reason: this term will pull in searches like 'which digital camera' and 'compare digital cameras'. People using a broad search term are likely to be in the early stages of choosing what to buy. Providing them with good content will help them make a buying decision. Note that they are unlikely to buy at this early stage of researching their options.

Modified broad match: +canon +digital +camera

Landing page: category page showing all your canon digital cameras.

Reason: someone searching for this term is likely to have moved further along the buying cycle to the point where they are considering a specific brand (such as 'Canon') but may not have chosen a particular model.

Exact match: [canon EOS 5D mark iv digital camera]

Landing page: product detail page showing the Canon EOS 5D Mark IV Camera.

Reason: someone searching for a particular model is likely to have a strong buying intent so you want to take them directly to the product page.

You need to decide whether you want to simply build your brand online, nurture potential customers through your funnel or simply attract customers ready to buy.

Writing your ad

Once you have set up your keywords and negative keywords, you need to create your ad. Writing a clear compelling ad, within the stipulated character limit, requires a lot of thought and most likely several attempts. You should always write three different ads and measure the performance of each one so you learn what works and what doesn't. This helps you to constantly hone your ads until they are as effective as they can possibly be.

Once you have created your ads you need to set your ad extensions. Ad extensions give you the ability to increase the marketing in your ad and your ad real estate. The current ad extensions are:

Sitelinks – you can add links to other pages of your site.

Flight Centre® Cambridge - Award-Winning Travel Agency
[Ad] www.flightcentre.co.uk/Flights/Economy ▼ 0800 280 8930
A Great Price & Expert Advice - Call Our Travel Experts For An Instant Quote!
Number 1 To Australia · Widest Choice Of Airfares · ATOL & ABTA Approved · Speak To An Expert
♀ 50 Sidney Street, Cambridge - Open today · 9:30 am – 6:00 pm ▼

| About Flight Centre | Tailor Made Holidays |
| Airfare Boosters | Find Your Local Store |

Callout – you can add an additional marketing message as a callout.

Flight Centre® Cambridge - Award-Winning Travel Agency
[Ad] www.flightcentre.co.uk/Flights/Economy ▼ 0800 280 8930
A Great Price & Expert Advice - Call Our Travel Experts For An Instant Quote!
Number 1 To Australia · Widest Choice Of Airfares · ATOL & ABTA Approved · Speak To An Expert
♀ 50 Sidney Street, Cambridge - Open today · 9:30 am – 6:00 pm ▼

About Flight Centre   Tailor Made Holidays
Airfare Boosters   Find Your Local Store

Structured snippets – you can list product types or brands that you stock.

eFlorist Flowers From £12.99 - Next Day Flower Delivery - eflorist.co.uk
[Ad] www.eflorist.co.uk/ ▼
4.1 ★★★★☆ rating for eflorist.co.uk
Flowers For All Occasions Delivered Next Day, Great Value, Fantastic Quality
Delivering Since 1947 · Order Now For Same Day · Same Day Flower Delivery
Styles: Handtied, Traditional, Contemporary, Modern

Flowers Under £30   Romantic Flowers
Same Day Flowers   Satisfaction Guaranteed

Call – you can add a telephone number.

Solicitors+cambridge - Delivering Excellent Service - barrellison.co.uk
[Ad] www.barrellison.co.uk/LegalServices ▼ 01223 417200
Long been associated with excellence of service in Cambridge. Call us.
♀ 39 Parkside, Cambridge - Open today · 9:00 am – 5:30 pm ▼

Litigation & Disputes   Personal Injury
Family Law & Divorce   Wills Probate Trusts Tax

This is particularly good for ads that appear on mobile devices, as the user can simply click the number in the ad to dial direct.

Message – allows people to contact you by text message (shown only to people on mobile phones). A prepopulated message will be sent to your business when the visitor taps the message icon.

Location – you can add your location to encourage people to visit your business.

Affiliate location – this is for larger manufacturers that sell their products through retailers. You can add the retailer's address or map to your ad.

Price – you can add 3-8 products/services with prices.

Review – you can add a review from a published source to your ad.

App – if you have an app you can have a link to the app in your ad.

This list is evolving and changing all the time, so make sure you stay on top of the Ad Extensions (and any other changes) to make sure you get the best out of your campaign and stay ahead of your competitors.

Budget

I often get asked what the budget for online paid advertising should be. Of course, this depends on your marketplace and many other variables, but do not expect to achieve much for less than £35 per day. Of course, many businesses say they want to spend as little as possible on paid advertising. What I have learnt over the past 15 years is that the clients who get the best results are the ones who invest in paid advertising with a view to achieving a good return on investment (ROI) or return on ad spend (ROAS). It is not unusual for our clients to achieve a ROAS of 250%.

While you can set up a Google AdWords account pretty quickly, you need to make sure you optimise your campaign so you don't end up paying more than you should for your ads.

Your position in the list of ads, and the price you pay, will be determined by a number of factors such as your quality score. To quote Google, "Quality score is an estimate of the quality of your ads, keywords and landing pages. Higher quality ads can lead to lower prices and better ad positions."[17]

Google don't say precisely how they calculate your quality score, but it is highly likely that it's based on these factors:

- Click through rate for a given keyword.

- Ad text relevance to the keyword.

- Landing page relevance to the keyword.

- Landing page speed.

As I said before, it all comes down to "follow the scent":

- Make sure your keyword is the term people are looking for.

- Use that keyword in your ad.

- Make sure the landing page is about the term that you used in your ad taking into account the intent.

- Make sure the landing page loads quickly.

- Make sure it is easy for the user to work out what to do next and that it is relevant to their intent.

Display ads

Google allows you to create different types of ads to appear on sites that are relevant to what you are selling. Google's display network reaches 90% of internet users so it is worth considering using Google Display for your business.

---

17 Google Adwords. (2017). *Quality Score Definition*. Retrieved from AdWords Help:
   https://support.google.com/adwords/answer/140351?hl=en-GB

9: It's wise to advertise

There are different formats for display ads: text, banner and video. The steps to set up display ads are:

- Pick a format and create your ad.

- Decide where your ad will show.

- Set your budget.

When selecting where you want your ads to show, you will be able to select from a number of targeting methods:

- Placement.

- Keyword.

- Topic.

- Audience.

- Remarketing.

- Combined targeting.

Placement targeting allows you to select which sites or specific pages of a site you want your ads to appear on.

Keyword targeting, as the name suggests, means your ad will appear on sites related to your keywords.

Topic targeting means your ad will only appear on sites about a particular topic — but there's a catch. The topics you are allowed to choose from are quite broad and so may not be specific enough to be very useful.

Audience targeting allows you to target audiences based on their interests. This is different from topic targeting as the ad is aimed at the user, not the content of the website they happen to be visiting. Suppose that Google knows, through the use of cookies, that Jane Smith is interested in wedding dresses. Jane could see your ad about your wonderful wedding dresses while she's visiting a site that has no direct relevance.

There are three types of audience targeting: affinity, custom affinity and in-market audiences.

Affinity audiences are defined by their interests.

Custom affinity audiences are defined by entering competitor URLs.

In-market audiences are people who are in the market for your products/services.

Google recently introduced audience targeting based on life events (marriage, moving house and so on), mobile purchases and app downloads. Google is still developing their range of audience targeting options, in an effort to compete with Facebook, and I expect even more options to be available in the future.

Figure 38: Display Ad on the Guardian

Figure 39: Display ad on The Telegraph

Remarketing targeting allows you to target people *after* they have visited your website — for example, they might see your ad when they are visiting a different website entirely. Remarketing can be simple or refined. In its simplest form, your ad gets shown to people based solely on the fact that they have visited your site at least once. In its more refined form, your ad gets shown to people who have visited your site and interacted with it in a predefined way — such as visiting particular pages or clicking on specific links.

Demographic targeting allows you to target people based on their age and gender, and can be applied to all interest and audience targeting. Much as I dislike gender-based targeting, if your audience is predominantly male, you may want to exclude women from your targeting.

Demographic targeting is something you may want to add to your campaign after you have been running it for some time. By analysing the performance of your campaigns, it may be clear that one or more specific demographic groups generate the best return on investment, allowing you to refine your targeting accordingly.

This is another feature that Google has introduced so they can compete with Facebook's targeting. Google has one big advantage over Facebook in that their browser, Chrome, is the most widely used browser in the world and most people are logged into Google when they browse. This means

Google has access to extensive behavioural and demographic data. Use this to your advantage.

Combined targeting

Combined targeting allows you to combine targeting methods, such as keywords and placements.

Test, measure and refine

For both search and display advertising, I recommend that you set up conversion tracking and measure your performance against your predefined goals. Constantly test your campaigns, measure the results and use the data to refine your marketing efforts.

Google Shopping Ads

If you are running an e-commerce store, I recommend that you run Google Shopping Ads. These are ads that display specifically when someone is searching for products with a clear intent to buy. The ad will consist of a product image, your price and your shop name. People who click on your ad will be taken directly to your e-commerce site where they can buy the item. You only pay Google when people click on the link.

While this kind of advertising is clearly useful for B2C marketing, some of our B2B clients also use it with great success. For example, one of our clients specialises in supplying electrostatic discharge products to the aerospace and electronics industry. They run shopping ads that generate sales month after month.

Setting up Google Shopping Ads is fairly straightforward:

1. Open a merchant centre account and link it with your Google AdWords account.
2. Create your product feed and make sure it contains all the relevant data required by Google.
3. Register your feed in your merchant centre.
4. Upload your products to your merchant centre account. Ideally, you want to set up an automated feed to ensure all your products and pricing is up-to-date.

Google has very clear policies regarding the data you upload to your feed. Make sure you comply with these requirements or your feeds may not work and your ads might not run.

Amazon ads

When I started writing this chapter I wasn't intending to cover Amazon ads at all. However, I was recently contacted by a client who felt they had to use Amazon ads to compete with a new threat: Chinese companies selling on Amazon in the UK.

Let's start with a brief summary of the different ways in which Amazon operates.

Amazon sellers are businesses and individuals that sell products on Amazon. They can ship the products themselves or use Fulfilment by Amazon (FBA) to fulfil customer orders. Sellers manage their inventory on Seller Central.

Amazon vendors are businesses that sell their products to Amazon — they are effectively suppliers to Amazon. Amazon vendors manage their inventory on Vendor Central.

If you are an Amazon vendor or seller, you may well want to consider their ad options. Amazon has a phenomenal share of the online shopping market. A 2016 survey showed some 55% of US online shoppers started their product searches on Amazon[18]. In 2017 a survey across the US, UK, Germany and France showed 56% of shoppers used Amazon as their starting point.[19]

There are three reasons you might want to use Amazon ads:

1. To help both sellers and vendors increase sales of their products on Amazon.

2. To drive Amazon traffic to your own website.

3. To help people discover your app on Amazon Fire and Android devices.

There are three different ad types for boosting product sales:

1. Sponsored products. These ads are keyword-targeted cost-per-click ads and allow you to advertise individual products that you sell. When someone clicks on your ad they will be taken to your product page on Amazon. These ads can appear both alongside and below search results, as well as on product detail pages.

2. Headline search ads are keyword-targeted cost-per-click ads that can show three or more products in an ad that appears above search results. When someone clicks on a

---

18 Rey, J. D. (2016, September 27). *55 percent of online shoppers start their product searches on Amazon*. Retrieved from Recode: *https://www.recode.net/2016/9/27/13078526/amazon-online-shopping-product-search-engine*

19 Sterling, G. (2017, Spetember 14). *Report: Google beats Amazon for product-search reach, but rival sees greater loyalty*. Retrieved from Search Engine Land: *https://searchengineland.com/report-google-beats-amazon-product-search-reach-rival-sees-greater-loyalty-282570*

headline search ad they will be taken to a brand page or custom landing page on Amazon.

3. Product display ads are cost-per-click product or interest targeted display ads that appear on the product detail page below the 'Add to basket' button.

Amazon have clear policies governing the use of these kinds of ads. Please familiarise yourself with these policies before you create your ad campaign.

Amazon uses keyword match types for keyword targeting. However, you need to review your choice of targeting on Amazon versus Google as the buying intent is likely to be different. For example, someone searching for 'digital camera' on Google is likely to be in the early, investigation stage of their buying journey. If they use the same keywords on Amazon they are more likely to be ready to buy.

Once you have set up your ads you will need to monitor how they perform and refine them over time. The only bad news is that the Amazon ad interface at ams.amazon.co.uk is truly frightful at the time of writing. I was assured by the Amazon team that the interface will improve over the next year!

Facebook ads

As I mentioned earlier, all the major social media websites offer advertising. I am focusing on Facebook because of its reach. One in every four minutes spent on mobile phones in the UK is spent on Facebook or Instagram.[20]

---

20 comScore. (2015). *Time spent on Smartphones UK.*

For B2B business, I generally recommend they confine their advertising to Google and LinkedIn. However, it's becoming clear that Facebook advertising can generate results for B2B too.

For B2C, I recommend Facebook and Google and, if your product is particularly visual, then Instagram and Pinterest too. If your demographic is 18-34, I also recommend Snapchat.

Facebook is in an unusual position because of its sheer popularity. Facebook enjoys 79% of the social media network market share in the UK[21] with 32 million users. Increasingly B2B buyers are using Facebook to make buying decisions. So, whether you are a B2B or B2C business, I now recommend running ads on Facebook.

5-step process for Facebook ads

Here's how to set up your Facebook ads:

1. Determine your objective, whether it's to increase sales, generate leads or increase brand or product awareness.

2. Target your audience using demographic, location and interest criteria.

3. Choose whether you want your ads to run on Facebook, Instagram or the apps and websites on their audience network.

---

21 StatCounter. (2016). *Social network market share held by Facebook in the United Kingdom (UK) from March 2014 to Ocotber 2016*. Retrieved from Statista: *https://www.statista.com/statistics/280301/market-share-held-by-facebook-in-the-united-kingdom-uk/*

4. Set your daily budget.

5. Create your ad using photo, carousel, video, slideshow or canvas formats.

Once your ads are up and running, you need to review their performance and make adjustments as required. This is an ongoing process. Don't run the same ad indefinitely on Facebook. You should aim to change your ads at least monthly. Make sure that you keep on top of the changes that the different platforms make in order to optimise your campaigns and to avoid overpaying for your ads.

Google v Facebook

Google AdWords[22]

- Average cost per click for B2B in the UK for search ads is £1.55 - £10.

- Average cost per click for B2B in the UK for display ads is £0.60 - £1.55.

- Average click-through rates for Google Search Ads is 1.91%.

- Average click-through rates for Google Display is 0.35%.

- Google Ads are currently easier to set up and manage than Facebook.

---

22 Wordstream. (2017). *Google AdWords Benchmarks for Your Industry Data*. Retrieved from Wordstream: *http://www.wordstream.com/blog/ws/2016/02/29/google-adwords-industry-benchmarks*

- Google Ads are suited to sales or lead generation as a searcher would normally signal intent.

Facebook ads

- The average cost per click for B2B in the UK is £0.15 - £1.55.[23]
- The average click-through rate for Facebook Ads is 0.9%.[24]
- Facebook Ads are suited to engagement and brand building.
- Facebook has a large potential audience.
- Strong audience targeting options but with lower buying intent.

The Nielson Norman Group recently conducted a study about attitudes to different ad formats and compared this to a study they conducted in 2004. Most people preferred ads that appeared on the right-hand side of the page, or among the related links at the bottom of the page.

The things that people hated in 2004 are still hated today! Fishburne offers this lovely summary of pet hates:

---

23 AdEspresso. (2016). *The Complete Resource to Understanding Facebook Ads Cost - 2016 Benchmarks.* Retrieved from AdEspresso: *https://adespresso.com/academy/blog/facebook-ads-cost/*

24 Wordstream. (2017). *Facebook Ad Benchmarks for your industry.* Retrieved from Wordstream: *http://www.wordstream.com/blog/ws/2017/02/28/facebook-advertising-benchmarks*

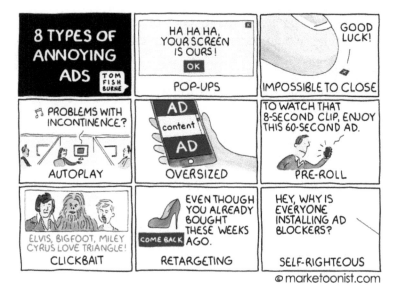

© marketoonist.com

The bottom line

- Not all businesses can take advantage of paid advertising, but those that can should consider it as a way of generating sales, engagement or brand awareness.

- Facebook ads can be a great way to increase brand awareness and increase engagement.

- LinkedIn ads can be a great way to increase engagement.

- Google ads can be a great way to increase leads and sales.

- Amazon ads are essential if you sell on Amazon.

- You don't have to pick one channel.

- Your ads need to be tailored to your channel.

- Make sure you keep on top of all the changes made by Google and Facebook.

- Test, measure and refine.

CHAPTER 10: THE FUN OF FUNNELS

Why automate?

Marketing automation enables you to automate some of your marketing based on predefined criteria. Good marketing automation can also be integrated with your customer relationship management (CRM) system, allowing you to measure the performance of your marketing right through to sales.

Conversion funnels

Conversion funnels are based on the premise that groups of customers behave differently depending on where they are in the buying cycle.

For example, suppose that someone is looking for information about how to choose a saxophone. If they get taken to a page where they can *buy* a saxophone, this won't achieve much because they aren't yet ready to make a purchase. Taking them to an information page that provides them with a buying guide, and *then* links them to a product page, would be a better option.

Generally, funnels have the following stages:

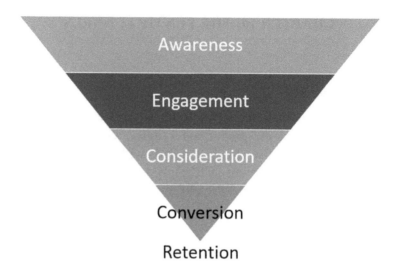

Awareness: this is where you create awareness about your business, product(s) or service(s). To do this you can use a combination of inbound and outbound techniques. Typical examples would be blog posts, cold traffic from Google AdWords, sponsored stories from LinkedIn, Facebook ads, YouTube ads, Instagram ads and social media campaigns.

Engagement: this is where your visitor has expressed an interest in what they saw/read in the awareness stage. You then offer them additional information in exchange for their email address. Typical examples would be giveaways, whitepapers, case studies and remarketing ads.

Consideration: this is where the visitor is considering what you offer. At this stage you would need to provide content that will help them make the buying decision. Typical examples would be demos, videos of products, product reviews or the option of a live chat to answer final questions.

Conversion: this is where you make the sale. This can be online or during a sales call.

Retention: this is where you have acquired the customer and you want to make sure they stay loyal.

Funnel example

Here's an example of a funnel that we created at Xanthos. The goal was to help Vigilant Software market their vsRisk software (a risk assessment tool).

We first defined that they had two key target personas, and we created persona profiles for both of them. One of them we called Infosec Manager Ian. We created a funnel intended to attract and engage Infosec Ian:

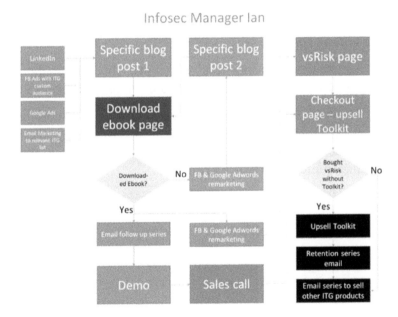

Having devised the funnel, we then worked with the client to define the blog posts, the ebook and the email campaigns. We made recommendations to improve the product page, the product pricing comparison page and the demo sign-up. We also created the download landing page using one of the highest-performing download layouts from a conversion point of view. We then wrote and set-up the ad campaigns. The impact of this funnel was that monthly sales increased tenfold within three months.

Your website might have multiple product or service ranges and multiple target personas. If this is the case, it might seem daunting to define multiple personas and funnels. It's a good idea to start with just one: choose your most important target persona, put the funnel in place, and then test and measure. You can then move on to the next product/service and target persona.

The bottom line

- Understand the positive difference that automation could make to your business and use it as appropriate.

- Increase conversions on your website by building specific conversion funnels for each of your target personas. If this seems a tall order, start with one and then build additional funnels.

CHAPTER 11: TREASURE THE MEASURE

The joy of data

The beauty of digital marketing is that it generates a wealth of data you can measure and analyse. Unlike offline marketing, where it's hard to measure a campaign's effectiveness, digital marketing allows you to measure performance with great accuracy.

However, you want to avoid generating so much data that you cannot see the wood for the trees. It's better to select a small number of the most significant indicators for your business and track them over time, since *trends* tell you far more than 'snapshot' figures from one point in time. There are a number of performance measurement tools available, but for smaller businesses I recommend Google Analytics.

Google Analytics

Overall analysis

Google Analytics provides a wealth of metrics in logical sections. You should set up Google Analytics to track the performance of your site and, if you have an e-commerce site, set up e-commerce tracking. You also need to define your goals (other than sales). For non-e-commerce sites, I recommend that you set up your lead conversion (often a thank you page following a completion of an online contact request) as your top conversion goal.

Audience

The dashboard shown in the Audience section provides a good snapshot of useful indicators regarding your site's usage and performance.

Sessions

Sessions measures the number of visits to your site for a given time period and the actions performed during those visits (for example, which pages the visitor clicked on). Note that the number of 'visits' is not necessarily the same as the number of 'visitors', since *one* visitor may be responsible for *several* visits.

Users

Users measures the number of visitors to your site for a given time period.

Pageviews

Pageviews measures the total number of pages viewed on your site for a given time period.

Pages/session

Pages/session shows the average number of pages viewed per session for a given time period.

Average session duration

Average session duration measures the average time spent on your site per session for a given time period. Bear in mind that this can only be measured where a visitor visits more than one page on your site.

I would normally expect a business to aim to increase the figures for the above five metrics (although they are lagging indicators) via their digital marketing and engagement activity.

Bounce rate

Bounce rate measures the rate at which visitors visit one page and then leave your site. The higher the figure, the worse it is. Bounce rates vary by industry and type of website, but the average is about 50%. Some types of pages tend to have higher bounce rates than others. For example, simple single action landing pages tend to have relatively high bounce rates.

New sessions

New sessions measures the percentage of first-time visits for a given time period. You can look at New v Returning to get a fuller picture. Both new and returning visits add value to a business. You want new visits to grow because this shows you are reaching new customers. However, you also want return visits to grow as this indicates customer loyalty. It is not unusual, depending on the industry, to see returning visits spend more than new visits. You will also need to look at this trend by device type.

Acquisition

One of the most important areas to focus on is the acquisition of traffic to your site and how well you meet your objectives for each of the channels.

The available data, combined with the costs of running your campaigns, should allow you to calculate your return on investment (ROI) for each channel.

One of the most useful reports is the source/medium report. This gives you the number of sessions from each type of channel, the number of new visitors, the bounce rate, pages/session, average session, conversions and conversion rates.

Make sure that all your campaigns are correctly tagged otherwise Google will lump anything it cannot ascribe to a source to Direct traffic.

It is probably also worth mentioning that you do not want to become over-reliant on any one channel. I still remember a horror story from my early days in the industry. A company had built up dominance for its chosen area on Google organic search results. Their sales were highly backend loaded for the Christmas season. In October one year, Google updated their algorithm with what became known as the Florida update. The Florida update devalued affiliate sites having keyword-stuffed domains with a network of keyword links pointing back to the home page. This also had an impact on the commercial sites the affiliates linked to. This company lost its rankings. They had no other marketing channels and their business did not survive.

Behaviour

The behaviour section gives you the ability to drill down into your content and measure how effectively it engages your visitors.

Review the Top Ten pages under the All Pages report and the Landing Pages report. For the Landing Pages report, I recommend that you review your landing pages by source. To do this you will need to create a secondary dimension for source/medium and use this to filter the results. This will enable you to review and evaluate the performance of your top SEO pages, top Google AdWords landing pages, top email marketing landing pages, and so on. You will then need to analyse the performance of each page to determine what action you can take to improve its performance.

If you are running an e-commerce site, review the on-site search using the Site Search report. This gives you useful information about the percentage of visits that use the site search, the conversion rate of visits with site search and the search terms people use on your site.

Conversions

Google Analytics allows you to set goals to measure the performance of your website. For example, one goal could be the completion of an enquiry form or requesting a brochure. The goals overview report will show you the number of goals completed in the period and the conversion rate for that goal.

For an e-commerce site, provided you have integrated your e-commerce site with the e-commerce tracking of Google Analytics, you can also measure the e-commerce conversion rate.

I normally recommend that you set up a funnel and measure the funnel stages. You can review the effectiveness of the funnel through the Funnel Visualisation report.

As discussed under Acquisition, the report that shows conversions by channel is a useful indicator of what works and what needs to be improved. One of the issues with this is the concept of attribution. Google attributes an action to the last source of entry to the site. Consider the following example. Someone sees your Google Ad, clicks through to your site and then leaves. They return the following day by clicking on one of your organic listings, and then decide to take a particular action such as filling in a form or buying something. Google will regard Google Organic as the source. In reality, both Google AdWords and Google Organic played a part in the final action. If you wish, you can select which attribution model you want to use for your report.

However, don't worry too much about these different attribution models. If you continue to monitor the trend of your conversions and source, using the standard 'last interaction' attribution model, and review assisted conversions, this is probably sufficient to create an accurate and useful analysis.

Data information insights

What I have outlined above is a summary of the data you should be looking at. However, for this to be meaningful you need to look at *trends*, such as comparing the current month with the previous month or the same month last year. You then need to analyse the data to obtain information. Too often I see what Avinash Kausik, a Google Analytics guru, terms 'data puking'[25]. This means reams of figures with no attempt to make sense of them, no analysis, no conclusions and no actionable insights.

To give you an example, in reviewing a client's Google Analytics I found a spike in organic traffic to their blog. To the uninitiated this might seem like good news. However, on further analysis, I found that most of this fresh burst of interest focused on one specific blog post. We cross checked

25 Kaushik, A. (2018). *Occam's Razor*. Retrieved from Occam's Razor: *https://www.kaushik.net/avinash/*

this with the search terms used (from the Google Search Console) and saw that one specific word, irrelevant to their business, was generating a very high number of impressions and clicks. This word appeared in the title of the blog post, which was why it was suddenly getting so many hits. This apparently promising spike in traffic had a high bounce rate and was in fact meaningless for the business. This client now knows how to target the terms they use for their blog posts far more accurately.

The lesson here is simple: don't just look at the numbers. Make sure you set relevant KPIs for your digital marketing and review them at least monthly. Analyse the data to glean information from which you can derive actionable insights.

Conversion rate optimisation

Conversion rate optimisation (CRO) is, as you might guess, the process of optimising a website, or part of a website, to increase conversions. A conversion can refer to anything from a particular action to a sale. Most businesses I work with want to improve conversions for either lead generation or sales, so I'll focus on these areas in this section.

The first step in CRO is to gather information. You can do this in a number of ways[26]:

- Use Google Analytics to analyse your pages and channels for conversions.

---

26 Quicksprout. (2017). *The Definitive Guide to Conversion Optimization.* Retrieved from Quicksprout: *https://www.quicksprout.com/the-definitive-guide-to-conversion-optimization/*

- Use heatmaps and visitor recordings.

- Use on-site surveys to ask your visitors about your site and what they would change.

- Run A/B tests.

Let's look at each of these in turn.

Google Analytics

Google Analytics provides useful data about how you are moving your customer through the steps in your conversion funnel. It should enable you to identify drop-off points and the pages where people have abandoned the funnel. For each drop-off point, consider technical aspects like page load times. Also assess the content of the page:

- Is it clear?

- Is it relevant?

- Is the next step in the journey clear?

There are a number of things you can do to improve page load times from compressing images to improving your hosting. For most businesses, you will need your developer to make these improvements.

For other page changes, you will have to assess what to change on the page, make the change and then measure the revised page's performance. Ideally, you want to do this with A/B testing.

Heatmaps

A heatmap is a visual representation of how visitors are using your site based on tracking mouse or touch movements. This should help you find out:

- Where most people look on the page.

- Where to place your calls to action.

- Whether your navigation is working.

- Whether the images/calls to actions are working.

Visitor recordings enable you to see exactly what a visitor does on your site. This data is not aggregated.

Typically, at Xanthos, we use Hotjar (*https://www.hotjar.com/*) for heatmaps and visitor recordings.

To create a heatmap, you simply add tracking code to your site (which you can do via Google Tag Manager). You can then set up heatmaps for particular pages on your site. Unlike Google Analytics, where you have to judge for yourself how to improve a particular page, heatmaps make it easy to see the specific hurdles people face. For example, one of our clients had a button at the bottom of an address input page saying 'Add address'. The designer thought the purpose of this button would be clear to the visitor — you've entered your address details, now simply press 'Add address' and your address will be updated. What we saw from visitor recordings was that people were scrolling up and down the page not knowing what to do. They were thinking, "I've already entered my address, I don't want to *add* another one!". We changed the button to say 'Save and continue'. This improved the conversion for that page by 11%.

Here is an example of how heatmap intelligence can work. We were about to design a new site for a client. While we knew the site needed a modern look and had to be mobile responsive, we wanted to know how visitors behaved on the current site before we built the new one. The results were very informative.

From the heatmap of the old homepage (shown below), you can see that many visitors (39%) were clicking on the central boxes while only 20% were clicking on the top navigation. In discussion with the client, we agreed that it would make sense to keep the central navigation boxes on the new site.

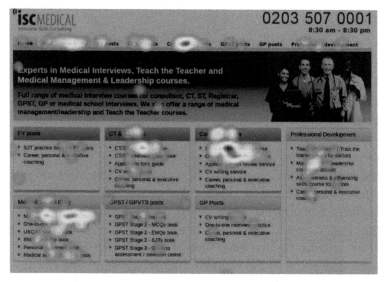

Figure 40: Heatmap of homepage before new design

We then looked at the product page of the client's most successful product. The original page was very long, so I have broken this up into three key findings.

First of all, we could see that, on a very long page, having intermittent 'Click here to buy' buttons worked well.

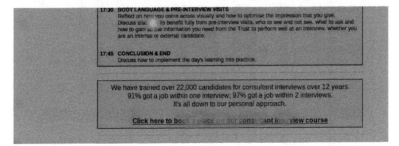

Figure 41: Heatmap of long product page with 'Click here to buy' button

The product we were looking at was a course that people could sign up for, and the page showed a calendar of available dates. From the heatmap, we could see that people were trying to click on the dates they wanted. This didn't work since the calendar was a non-clickable static display. We therefore recommended that the client incorporate an interactive calendar on the course pages.

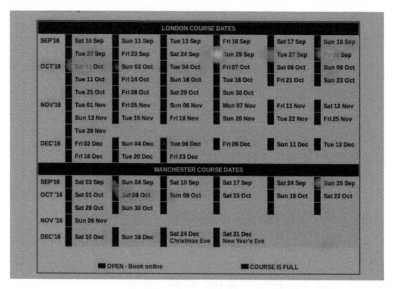

Figure 42: Heatmap of static calendar

Right at the bottom of the product page was the 'Buy' box. Despite being right at the bottom of the page, we could see this was the highest click area. We knew that this page had a conversion rate of 3.85% with a page value of £17.82. Our objective was to see whether we could improve on this.

Figure 43: Heatmap of buy box

Following the launch of the new site, the conversion rate of this product page improved 114%, to 8.27%. The page value increased 102%, to £36.05.

A/B Testing

A/B testing involves running two versions of one page to see which one performs better. You can set up your test environment so that both versions of the page get displayed equally often. After a period of time, you will be able to see which version of the page works best. There are several A/B testing tools available, but Visual Website Optimiser (*https://vwo.com/*) is a reasonable price for an SME.

A word of warning: if your visitor volume is low, A/B testing may not be very useful. You need sufficient data to produce a statistically significant result. Opitmizely has a calculator[27] that shows you the sample size required for different rates of conversion. For example, if your control page is converting at 3% and you want a 20% uplift with a 95% certainty that the change will produce the effect, known as significance, then you need a sample size of 13,000.

Customer surveys

On-site surveys are a good way to get customers to give feedback. There are a number of tools that offer this service (Hotjar, SurveyMonkey, Qualaroo, etc.). Surveys are another way of getting direct feedback on what you can improve on your site. Avinash Kaushik summed up the best questions to ask on a survey:

---

27 Optimizely. (2017). *A/B Test Sample Size Calculator*. Retrieved from Optimizely: *https://www.optimizely.com/sample-size-calculator/*

- What was the purpose of your visit today?

- Were you able to complete the purpose of your visit today?

- If you were not able to complete the purpose of your visit today, why not?[28]

Of course, you can ask other questions depending on when you trigger the survey — as a thank you page or on a first page for new visitors, etc.[29]

To summarise: once you are up and running you need to continuously test, measure and refine your customer journey to improve their experience, making it easier for them to buy from you or fill out that vital lead form. This, in turn, will improve your return on investment from your website and your digital marketing.

The bottom line

- Use data to make informed decisions about changes to your website.

- Use Google Analytics.

- Use heat mapping tools.

- Use visitor recordings.

---

28 Kaushik, A. (2017). *The Three Greatest Survey Questions Ever.* Retrieved from Occam's Razor: *http://www.kaushik.net/avinash/the-three-greatest-survey-questions-ever/*

29 Survicate. (2017). *The 20 most popular website survey questions.* Retrieved from Survicate: *https://survicate.com/website-survey/questions/*

- Use A/B testing tools if you get enough visitors to make it worthwhile.

- Use surveys to gather feedback.

- Continuously evaluate and improve your customer journey to achieve better conversion rates.

CHAPTER 12: OUTSOURCE? OF COURSE!

A new profession

Digital marketing has exploded over the past 15 years. It is now a fully-fledged profession with a constantly growing body of knowledge, like accountancy, production management or any other technical discipline. Typically, a business that wants to manage its own digital marketing needs to master all of the following skills:

- Digital marketing strategy development.
- Funnel development.
- Content creation.
- Design for websites, email campaigns, display adverts, landing pages and social media branding.
- Google AdWords, Bing Ads, Facebook Ads, Twitter Ads and LinkedIn Ads.
- Social media marketing.
- Measurement and analysis.
- Conversion rate optimisation.
- HTML and CSS coding.
- SEO skills.

The business has to do all these things while competing against other companies who are simultaneously striving to improve *their* digital marketing.

Different sized companies have different problems:

12: Outsource? Of course!

Big companies need to have the competency of building the best web, digital marketing and e-commerce teams in their competence set.

Medium-sized companies need to be able to manage the core elements internally and supplement in-house expertise with one or more specialists.

Smaller companies may not have the resources to recruit and manage people who are sufficiently experienced, or good enough, to deliver a profitable return on investment and activities. They will almost certainly need to rely on external expertise.

Start-ups often have to learn the ropes themselves or find other low-cost resources to help them get to first base.

At Xanthos, we have developed a model of working called outsourced digital marketing. We work as the specialist department for growing businesses. This gives the business owner the ability to see results and return on investment without the risk of learning about digital marketing from scratch or investing in one person who turns out to be less effective than was hoped.

Increasingly, small businesses are finding it harder to set up and manage digital marketing themselves. This is why I have included this chapter on outsourcing digital marketing.

Outsourcing your digital marketing needs to an agency that understands your business yields three major benefits:

1. You save on the cost of marketing your business.

2. You free up your internal resources to focus on your core competencies.

3. Your business benefits from marketing expertise.

12: Outsource? Of course!

Save money by outsourcing your digital marketing

The big consideration when weighing up your options is the cost. Outsourcing your digital marketing costs a fraction of what it would take to hire your own team of professionals and achieve the same level of expertise.

The cost to hire at least five industry experts can be a huge investment for many businesses. Even if the average salary were £25k a year, you'd be spending over £125k a year just on your digital marketing. Outsourcing this to an agency will cost less than half for a comprehensive digital marketing package — and you will have access to seasoned experts.

For most small business, even hiring just a couple of in-house marketing specialists simply isn't feasible or appropriate.

Partnering with a digital agency is **less than half the cost of hiring an in-house team.** Outsourced digital marketing packages tend to start at around £1,000 a month, rising to around £5,000 per month depending on your requirements. You can see why, just from a cost perspective, outsourcing your digital marketing makes sense.

Other than the initial savings, you also don't have any of the worries or cost of training your staff. This can include continuous professional training, certifications, conferences and time to stay on top of new developments regarding matters such as SEO, PPC, social media and other forms of paid advertising.

Another consideration is the management and recruitment costs of hiring your own marketing team. What happens when a member of your team is on holiday, or on maternity leave? Outsourcing your digital marketing to an agency means you aren't left vulnerable when your staff members are absent.

Big businesses may already have a marketing department, but still often benefit from an outside agency. A good digital agency will act as another arm of your marketing department, helping to improve the performance of your current marketing, suggesting areas of improvement, and supplementing your internal skill set.

As the online marketplace evolves, as well as marketing techniques, it can be expensive for businesses to adopt new tools in order to stay ahead online. Any decent digital agency will have access to an array of tools to help their clients, which saves you the cost of investing in the tools yourself.

Benefit from seasoned marketing experts

Agency marketers work in a dynamic environment, which requires them to update their skills and stay on top of the latest trends. Also, agencies have gained expertise in marketing for similar businesses in various industries, meaning they have added knowledge that can benefit your business.

If you're considering keeping your marketing in-house, consider the fact that almost half of 1000 small business owners surveyed by Infusionsoft and Leadpages[30] said they don't know if they are marketing themselves effectively. In fact, 14% stated that they know they *aren't*.

Keeping in-house staff up-to-date requires time and training. You constantly need to identify the training your staff need

---

30 *http://leadpages.s3.amazonaws.com/2016%20Small%20Business%20Marketing%20Trends%20Report.pdf*

in order to keep your business ahead, then organise it and pay for it. With an agency, you don't have these problems.

For instance, staying on top of SEO is not as simple as it seems. While most businesses understand the importance of keywords, and the need to keep their website up-to-date, these measures alone aren't enough to stay ahead of their competitors. An agency will be on top of what Google has in store, whether it's algorithm updates or alterations to the search experience. This insight can help you push ahead with your SEO and digital marketing expertise in areas where your competitors will not. This gives you a great advantage in gaining the best possible quality traffic from organic search results, to help your business generate sales.

Agencies will also have specialist staff who are experts in different fields, ensuring your business benefits from the best and most up-to-date knowledge in each area of digital marketing. The right digital agency can draw on past experience building campaigns or developing marketing strategies that get results, and find the best solution for your unique business needs.

Free your internal resources

How often does your team not deliver the marketing materials or campaigns they were supposed to? Staff with numerous responsibilities may feel pressured and overwhelmed when they cannot deliver on marketing targets. This leads to an uncomfortable working atmosphere which is ultimately not good for your business.

Marketing is often neglected due to limited internal resources, which means staff cannot cope with the workload. By outsourcing your digital marketing to an experienced agency, you can relieve the pressure on your in-house staff and free your internal resources to be focused elsewhere.

Ascend2 found that **70% of B2B organisations outsource all or part of their digital marketing tactics, primarily the most difficult types to execute.**[31]

Outsourcing allows you and your team to focus on your core business competencies. Instead of your staff being spread too thinly across different areas of the business, outsourcing allows them to concentrate on the areas where they will make the best use of their time.

It's likely you're not an expert in developing a marketing strategy and deploying online marketing campaigns that bring in leads and generate sales. Outsourcing activities that are not your core competencies, such as digital marketing, makes sense. This way you can be assured you have digital marketing experts dedicated to your marketing, while you focus on what you know best.

Agencies are not just there to do the work you don't have the capabilities to do. A digital marketing agency can become your digital marketing department, forming an important partnership that helps to enhance your business's performance.

The bottom line

- Understand the value of outsourcing your digital marketing to professionals.

- Find the best, most co-operative way to work in *partnership* with your digital marketing agency.

---

31 http://mktg.actonsoftware.com/acton/attachment/248/f-1c46/1/-/-/-/-
/Ascend2_State%20of%20Digital%20Marketing_SMB.pdf

12: Outsource? Of course!

- Focus on what you do best (running your business) and let your agency 'take the strain' of devising and implementing the ideal digital marketing strategy.

CASE STUDIES

Here are some examples of how Xanthos has helped its clients.

IT Governance

In 2005, cyber security specialists IT Governance were just a start-up. By their own admission, they knew little about digital marketing. We advised them on their digital and e-product strategy development, developed their first e-commerce website and helped them with search engine optimisation. We also helped them with their email marketing strategy. With our help, they were able to generate online sales in the first month and continued to grow their customer base and online sales all through their first year. Later, we managed their Google AdWords account and developed their social media marketing strategy.

Today, the company has a dedicated digital marketing team while we continue to manage their Google AdWords campaigns and develop their e-commerce websites. These websites include complex customisations that improve both the customer experience and business efficiency. We also provide monthly reports on the performance of their websites. By 2017, IT Governance had achieved turnover of £7m and was able to successfully float on the London AIM market (their ticker symbol is GRC if you want to look it up).

ISC Medical

In 2004, ISC Medical was a start-up in the medical interview coaching market. In 2005, when they were turning over £250K, we implemented a search engine optimisation strategy that transformed their website rankings. As a result, they doubled their turnover in just four months. We subsequently built their e-commerce sites and automations to improve their administrative efficiency and continue to provide digital marketing services. Their turnover has grown from £250K to £1.5m.

Normans Musical Instruments

Normans Musical Instruments, as the name suggests, is a leading musical instrument retailer. They were an established 'bricks and mortar' company that decided to start selling online. We started working with them in 2011, developing a new e-commerce website that automatically feeds their different marketing channels and is fully integrated with their accounting system. They have a small in-house marketing team that we work with more or less constantly. We provide strategic direction for their search engine optimisation, content, marketing automation and both Google AdWords and Amazon Ads campaigns. The company's online turnover has grown 72% in the last 3 years.

ABOUT XANTHOS

Xanthos is a digital marketing agency that specialises in helping small- and medium-sized businesses increase their profits through the strategic development and implementation of digital marketing.

We work with managing directors and CEOs of small- and medium-sized businesses who know that digital marketing is key to their business success. We are committed to gaining an understanding of each client's specific business need. We couple this with our expertise in digital marketing to generate results that make a significant, positive difference to each client's business.

We have also devised a Digital Marketing Quotient to help managing directors and CEOs evaluate the digital marketing standing of their businesses. You can access this here:

https://www.e-xanthos.co.uk/digital-marketing-quotient

We also design and build websites for businesses, with particular strength in e-commerce websites customised to meet specific market needs.

You can stay up to date with the latest developments in digital marketing by signing up to our newsletter:

https://www.exanthos.co.uk/newsletter